RAISING BACKYARD CHICKENS

A BEGINNER'S GUIDE TO A HEALTHY FLOCK, BOOSTING EGG PRODUCTION, AND FRESH EGGS FOR LIFE!

DANIEL A. HART

© Copyright 2021 - **All rights reserved.**

The content contained within this book may not be reproduced, duplicated or transmitted without direct written permission from the author or the publisher.

Under no circumstances will any blame or legal responsibility be held against the publisher, or author, for any damages, reparation, or monetary loss due to the information contained within this book. Either directly or indirectly. You are responsible for your own choices, actions, and results.

Legal Notice:

This book is copyright protected. This book is only for personal use. You cannot amend, distribute, sell, use, quote or paraphrase any part, or the content within this book, without the consent of the author or publisher.

Disclaimer Notice:

Please note the information contained within this document is for educational and entertainment purposes only. All effort has been executed to present accurate, up to date, and reliable, complete information. No warranties of any kind are declared or implied. Readers acknowledge that the author is not engaging in the rendering of legal, financial, medical or professional advice. The content within this book has been derived from various sources. Please consult a licensed professional before attempting any techniques outlined in this book.

By reading this document, the reader agrees that under no circumstances is the author responsible for any losses, direct or indirect, which are incurred as a result of the use of the information contained within this document, including, but not limited to, — errors, omissions, or inaccuracies.

CONTENTS

Introduction	vii
1. RAISING CHICKENS: IS IT RIGHT FOR YOU?	1
Advantages of Raising Chickens	3
Disadvantages of Raising Chickens	11
Frequently Asked Questions	19
2. HOUSING AND CHICKEN COOP REQUIREMENTS	23
Why a Coop Is Important	24
Nesting Boxes: Their Role and Importance	28
So You Want to Build a Coop?	32
Buying a Premade Coop	39
Building from Scratch	39
Chicken Tractors	46
Tips for Building a Successful Coop	46
Bedding Materials	48
Cleaning Your Coop	54
3. SELECTING THE RIGHT BREED	57
Hen Breeds	58
Rooster Breeds	77
Sourcing Chicks	88
What Is a Broody Hen?	91
4. PROVIDING THE PROPER NOURISHMENT	94
Starter Diets	97
Grower Diets	98
Finisher Diets	98
Layer Diets	99
Making Natural Feed	100

Frequently Asked Questions	101
Hydrating Your Chickens	108
5. TIME TO BRING HOME THE BABIES	114
Building a Brooder	115
The Day Of Arrival	124
Signs Of Sickness	125
Introducing Your Chick to the Rest of the Flock	126
6. EGGS 101	129
Training Your Hens to Use Nesting Boxes	130
When And How Often to Collect Eggs	131
Cleaning, Storing, and Refrigerating Eggs	132
Preparing Eggs for Sale	134
Egg Shortage and How to Correct It	136
7. CHICKEN BEHAVIOR AND TROUBLESHOOTING	142
Dust Baths & Why They Do It	143
How to Stop a Chicken from Eating Eggs	144
Mating	147
Roaming	148
Preening	149
Scratching	149
Pecking Order	150
Helping an Egg-Bound Hen	150
8. HEALTH CONCERNS AND REMEDIES	157
Chicken First-Aid Kit	158
Caring for a Sick or Injured Chicken	160
Common Chicken Diseases and Parasites	163
Please Review My Book	171
FINAL WORDS	173
Also by Daniel A. Hart	177
About the Author	179
References	181

JUST FOR YOU FOR BUYING MY BOOK

BONUS GIFTS TO MY READERS...

Bonus #1: Sustainable Living: Amish Recipes From Home
Bonus #2: Access to Color Images From All Books
Bonus #3: Goat Log Worksheet
Bonus #4: Chicken Egg Log Worksheet

Visit the link:

Daniel-hart.com

INTRODUCTION

"No matter where I go, I'll never forget home. I can feel its heartbeat a thousand miles away. Home is the place where I grew my wings."

-Brenda Sutton Rose

Every summer around May, my family got a batch of baby chicks. My siblings and I always raised these helpless animals. Dad built an area for them in the barn until they were old enough to be on their own. Every day, I would hunker in front of these chicks, feeding them, watering them, and ensuring that the temperature was just right. In the morning, when I went into the barn, the chicks, cows, ducks, horses, and donkeys would greet me hungrily, relieved to see me—it was very loud before feeding time. I always fed them well, grateful for their service on the farm and for providing us with constant nourishment every day. Without them, we could not survive.

When they were old enough, we would let them out every morning, free to roam. They loved to forage for worms, bugs, and grit, clucking happily whenever they found a fat, juicy bug.

Looking back on it, country life was a dream, and it has inspired billions of people throughout history. The bubbling brook, fresh air, green spaces, and low hum of local animals enjoying their place on Earth—these are, no doubt, some of the images that have motivated you to want to start raising backyard chickens. You want to grow closer to nature, eat healthier, and discover that unbreakable bond between animal and master.

In a world of rapid urbanization, isolation, and individualization, it is no surprise that so many of us want to work the land again. We want to return to our agricultural roots. This is reflected in the studies of poultry scientists Elkhoraibi et al., which show the increasing popularity of keeping backyard chickens in the United States (2014).

I grew up in an Amish community until I was eighteen. I then chose to travel the United States before settling down closer to family. The Amish are not afraid of hard work—they live off the land and away from the distractions of big city life as much as possible. Though I am no longer Amish, their core values still resonate with me, and they have carried me through much of my life.

Throughout my childhood, I worked with, trained, and spent time with a wide variety of farm animals. I gained experience growing my own food by working in the fields, tending to our gardens, and preserving and canning food. I also worked for an Amish construction company, which taught me detailed carpentry work and how to frame, roof, and remodel homes.

My skills never left me. I used them everywhere I went as I traveled and learned about new cultures. Even after returning closer to home, settling down, and leaving my old lifestyle behind, I found it important to incorporate the ethics of self-sufficiency that had once defined me. Nature never left me, and I could not leave nature behind, either.

Growing up Amish, I learned that the Earth provides everything we need to survive and that it is our job to nurture the Earth and its riches so we can reap the rewards of our hard work. I learned to view our farm animals as functional tools for survival: our horses pulled, our chickens laid eggs and produced meat, and our cows produced milk. However, during my travels, I met other farming communities like mine, where farmers shared a special bond with their animals. At first, this shocked me. I would never had the luxury of seeing my animals as pets because the Amish lifestyle is one of hard work and survival. However, I began to see that farm animals can provide emotional support that is just as important to survival as the food and hard work that they produce. Today, I am an avid lover of chickens for their nutritious eggs and delicious meat, the entertainment they bring me, and the special and unique bonds that I share with each of them.

In this book, you will learn the advantages and disadvantages of raising chickens, why coops are essential for chickens, and how to properly set up an enclosure in your backyard. I will guide you on how to protect your hens from predators, how to encourage hens to produce plenty of eggs, and what rooster breeds are available to you as a beginner backyard chicken enthusiast. This book brings you tips to help you increase egg production, take good care of your chickens, and become self-sufficient while doing so.

Raising Backyard Chickens is a beginner's guide for those who want to start raising chickens at their homes. It will cover common questions from beginners, giving you the knowledge and the confidence to raise chickens in your own backyard.

This is your first step in becoming one of the many households in the United States raising backyard chickens. Enjoy the process!

As a thank you to my readers, I am offering you access to all the color photographs in this book. Simply follow the link on the 'Just for Buying My Book' page and click to subscribe to emails. You will receive an email link to a PDF that grants you access to colored versions of all pictures in this book, as well as any future books from me.

ONE

RAISING CHICKENS: IS IT RIGHT FOR YOU?

"I began raising chickens primarily for their eggs, but over the years, I've also grown fond of caring for them and learning about their many different breeds and varieties."

-Martha Stewart

Is raising chickens right for you? This is the most critical question to consider as you power through this book.

In the United States, we produce approximately 100 billion eggs in over 233 thousand locations annually. We love chickens and eggs so much that we have made it into a 50 billion dollar industry, nine percent larger than it was in 2013. In 2017, 22.85 billion chickens in the world (Statista, 2021).

You love chickens, you love eggs, and you wonder if you can raise chickens, too. You may wonder, why not? Raising chickens is like raising any other pet. Nobody denies how cute puppies are, but caring for them is, undoubtedly, a big responsibility. Caring for chickens is a big responsibility in the same sense. They require work, supplies, and commitment to ensure that they are happy and productive.

The first things to consider before you begin to raise chickens are the advantages and disadvantages of this incredible undertaking. Here is a list of pros and cons to help you make an informed decision that is right for your needs and circumstances.

Advantages of Raising Chickens

Loving Pets

Chickens don't have an excellent reputation as loving pets, even though they can be. The myth of the cranky chicken, squawking angrily at its owners, is only that—a myth. Chickens are loving, loyal pets that can become attached to their owners. Chickens are known for their unique personalities and quirky nature among poultry farmers. They are well-regarded for their "funny antics" (Kelly, 2012) and, indeed, for being as emotionally supportive as any dog, cat, bird, or other pet can be.

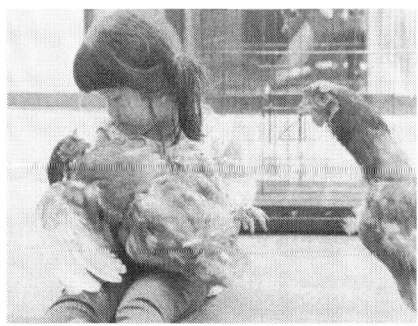

Here is a funny excerpt from a blogger who paints a wonderful picture of the joy of raising chickens as pets:

"When we first embarked upon our journey as chicken keepers, I was rather sanguine about what would happen when the hens stopped laying eggs (typically they lay 2–3 years). We planned to just "re-home" the chicken and replace it with another. After two years, I am not sure I can say the same thing!

Astrid, a Blue Andalusian, is the boss of the hen house, she definitely rules the roost. Miss Lemon, a Buff Cochin, has a huge butt and waddles around the yard with a jaunty step. Penny, a Welsummer is the quietest of the bunch and great for kids to cuddle. And Ruby, an Ameraucana, is the most reliable egg layer of the bunch, even if she does look more masculine than most. As you consider bringing chickens into your own lives, keep in mind they may have a greater impact on your well-being than just providing great eggs. These girls also support an emotionally positive lifestyle and help contribute to your individual mental health!" (Kelly, 2012)

As described above, chickens can possess unique personalities. While one may be feisty, another might be shy. While one may be grumpy or irritable, another might be sweet and loving. Essentially, you will not be bored when you have chickens around as pets.

. . .

Delicious, High-Quality Eggs

As your pets, chickens can spend all day roaming freely, eating the best feed, and enjoying life with minimal stress. Your hens can regularly lay fresh, delicious, and nutrient-laden eggs. This means that you and your family can enjoy the best chicken eggs that nature has to offer. Freshly-laid eggs taste much better than factory-farm hens. Thanks to the delicious eggs that my hens produce, breakfast is now solidified as the day's most important meal.

Moreover, you can control what goes into your eggs. I feed my hens good quality produce filled with vitamin A and vitamin E. This ensures that they produce eggs laden with the same nutritious vitamins. Chickens also love to eat table scraps, as well as bugs, weeds, and so on. Such a diet will result in the best eggs you have ever tasted.

Usually, chickens lay one egg per day, although some lay three to four per week. Depending on your daily egg needs, you may even have too many eggs to finish. You can sell these eggs at farmer's markets or to neighbors, friends, local restaurants, and so on. You can likely sell these eggs for an excellent price, as truly free-range, organic, local eggs are a specialty worldwide. If you have willing children, you can have them sell the eggs as an exercise in entrepreneurship.

Self-Sufficiency

Raising chickens might seem like a daunting task at first, but the more skilled you become, the more your confidence will rise. Part of this increase in confidence is gaining a new skill: self-sufficiency. Raising chickens will allow you to produce and grow your own food in a world that relies heavily on industrialized, impersonal farming and agricultural practices such as battery farming and factory farming.

Not only will you be able to become self-sufficient, but you will also be able to become one with nature. By learning how to care for other animals, you will be adding more to nature rather than taking from it. You will participate in the joys of taking care of another living being and watching it thrive as a result of your efforts. You will bond with other living things who, in turn, will also connect with you.

Bug, Weed, and Pest Killer

Chickens love to eat bugs and weeds. This is great for your house, yard, and garden because the chicken will keep it tidy and pristine. You do not need to use insecticides or pesticides because your chicken will spend all day searching for grasshoppers, snails, slugs, ladybugs, and all sorts of creepy crawlies. Do not worry if a fruit falls from its stem—your pet will be there to devour it before it attracts bugs and other nuisances. These multi-purpose pets even act as leftover vacuums, eager to eat all the scraps and leftovers from your daily meals. Chickens love vegetable peels, fruits, seeds, nuts, and many other scraps. Let them eat as much as they want—these scraps will lead to quality, delicious eggs.

Not only do chickens clear your yard of weeds, but they will also kill mice, small snakes, and other pests that venture into your yard. If a snake slithers into your property, it may be looking for chicken eggs. A full-grown chicken isn't an easy meal for a local snake.

Although it may take a few swipes of her beak for a hen to kill a snake, they can move incredibly fast with their beaks. Chickens are also a flock animal, so if they notice one chicken trying to kill a snake, the rest will flock towards the snake to kill it.

Excellent Fertilizers

Chicken manure is one of the best animal manures on the planet. Once properly composted, chicken manure releases potassium, nitrogen, and phosphorus into your soil. Do not use fresh chicken manure, however. I typically wait for the waste to compost for a month before adding it to my compost heap. I also add all of the dry leaves and shavings in my coop into my compost heap. If you want to use chicken manure, you will have to make sure that your chickens have a coop with bedding where they can sleep every night. If you allow them to roam freely, they will relieve themselves everywhere, meaning that you cannot easily collect their manure once a month—unless you want to leave it dotted around your yard.

. . .

Delicious Meat

This is arguably one of the best advantages of keeping a chicken: once in a while, you may get a craving for fresh, free-range, organic fried chicken. Homegrown chicken is much healthier; it contains less fat, calories, hormones, pesticides, and antibacterials. Best of all, it is more delicious.

There may be moments where you have bonded too closely with your pets and are unable to slaughter them for meat. If this is the case, it may be best not to get too close to your chickens if you plan to use them for meat at a later date.

Cheap And Easy

The decision to raise chickens can be cheap or expensive, depending on your motives and your method. It is very affordable to purchase chicks. For example, baby chicks are available for six dollars apiece. Installing a chicken coop is also easy and straightforward; most coops come pre-built and can be purchased for less than 200 dollars. Likewise, feeding a chicken is budget-friendly because they, in turn, provide you with regular food and can bring in revenue through eggs, chicks, or meat. Compared to other pets, chickens are cheap, easy to raise, and do not require too much attention, making them an ideal pet for anyone on a budget. You also do not need too much space when taking care of a chicken. A small or medium backyard is more than enough space for a few chickens to roam happily.

Lucrative

As chickens do not need much equipment or care to survive, chicken care is relatively inexpensive. As long as they live in a coop and are provided with plenty of shade, food, and water, chickens will do fine. If you prefer, you can start a chicken farm. Broiler chickens, for example, reach adulthood after a couple of months. You can keep some eggs from the first batch to hatch, sell the rest of the first batch for profit, and begin the process over again. Breeding free-range chickens for profit offers a good return on a one-time investment.

Mental Health

As already mentioned above, you can very easily find yourself bonding with your pets. Most research concludes with the same findings: our pets enhance our physical and mental health. Caring for pets can lower your blood pressure, slow your heart rate, reduce stress and stress hormones (like cortisol), increase your self-esteem and well-being, and make us feel needed (Newport Academy, 2021). When you stroke or snuggle with your pet(s), your breathing becomes more regular, and muscle tension relaxes. Animals are so beneficial for our mental health that we now have animal-assisted therapy programs. Your new pets may be a rich source of improving your mental health, possibly resulting in a healthier, happier you.

Healthy Chickens

Raising backyard chickens can produce healthy chickens and healthy eggs. Chickens thrive in nice backyards because they have everything they need: weeds, plants, mobility, sunshine, shade, water, great food, love, affection, bugs, and a clean environment.

Elise (2017) said:

> "Since I started [keeping free-range chickens], I have never had an overweight chicken. Even my bigger breeds like my Brahmas tend to stay quite fit because they get plenty of exercise roaming around the farm all day. They stay healthier because they are not living in close quarters [like a coop] and are at less risk of catching illnesses [like respiratory problems or avian flu] they may be exposed to in a coop setting. If I have a bird get sick, it's typically one bird... Most of the time, I can catch it and quarantine that individual [bird] to treat her instead of having to treat the whole flock. Most medications on the market today have a withdrawal period, meaning the eggs laid by that bird must be tossed. So, treating a lone individual is much more conve-

nient than having to treat my entire flock and buy eggs from the store."

Research has shown that free-range chickens lay eggs higher in Omega-3 fatty acids and lower in cholesterol (Anderson, 2011). This is because free-range eggs have better access to grass, green leaves, and insects. Even chickens not allowed to roam free in your backyard will provide better-tasting and healthier eggs than store-bought varieties. If you must keep your chickens in a coop, there are still ways to adjust their food to produce nutritious, great-tasting eggs. These methods will be discussed in Chapter Four.

Disadvantages of Raising Chickens

Noise

Chickens are very noisy pets. The rooster is iconic for its loud, relentless "cock-a-doodle-doo" wake-up call every morning. When you need to sleep in, or you are sick or tired, this is the last thing you want to hear. Unfortunately, this noise is not limited to once per day; chickens are consistently noisy. Some hens may also let out a "cock-a-doodle-doo" at any time of day.

After laying eggs, hens are also prone to celebrate with loud noises and squawks. Indeed, chickens may also fight or taunt each other occasionally, causing a ruckus among all your poultry pets. Chickens who are genuinely free-range hate being in their coop and may vocally complain when this happens. As naturally noisy animals, your neighbors might not appreciate you having chickens as pets.

Cleaning

Although chicken manure is highly beneficial, chickens leave droppings everywhere—even in their coop. Prepare to step in manure frequently. You will need to clean up the backyard and coop often to keep it clean and tidy. Furthermore, chickens themselves need to be cleaned regularly. It is also necessary to clean their bedding material often, which will be discussed in Chapter Two.

Feeding

If you want to raise organic chickens, you can feed them leftover food and scraps from your meals, as long as you eat a balanced diet yourself. Bread, corn, grains, oatmeal, vegetables, and fruits are safe for chicken consumption. My chickens love to eat raw vegetables.

Raw potato peels, large amounts of salt, spoiled or rotten foods, coffee or coffee grounds, citrus fruits, soft drinks, chocolate, greasy foods, and processed foods can be toxic or unhealthy for your chicken. Avoid feeding your chickens garlic, onions, and other strong-tasting foods, as they affect the way your chickens' eggs taste.

Nonetheless, you will still need to feed them organic chick starter, crumbles, and layer pellets (though the layer pellets come later). Chickens also need to be fed grit, which is a mixture of small rocks that helps them digest their food. I let them roam around in my backyard every day. They eat the stones around my backyard, so they do not need as much store-bought grit. Organic chicken feed is high in protein, allowing your chickens to lay great eggs and have good feathers. This may cost you about thirty dollars a month, which you can recoup by selling eggs.

On the other hand, once your chickens stop laying eggs, they can live for fifteen more years, costing you money and time without the added benefit of laying eggs. Indeed, once hens mature, they become tough and hard to cook and eat. If you have ten hens, for example, you will need to spend money and time taking care of them for many years after they stop laying eggs. You will need to continue to feed them scraps, vegetable peelings, supplements, seeds, and so on to keep them healthy. This will become expensive in the long run. In addition, you may want to buy younger chickens to produce more eggs, costing you more money.

Hens only lay eggs for a two to three-year period. If you are not able to part with your hen after this period because you have bonded with her, then you will be spending a lot of time, money, and effort on a chicken that no longer produces food, and that may be too old to be sold for meat. You must be prepared and ready to spend money on your chickens as pets that give nothing in return but friendship, companionship, and loyalty.

Chickens Can Be Mean

Although they can be loyal, friendly companions, chickens can also bully each other severely. There is some truth in the myth of mean chickens. They have been known to peck each other until they bleed, sometimes pecking a defenseless chicken to death. However, you cannot keep just one chicken because chickens are social animals, and they have been known to die of loneliness.

Disease and Health

Like all animals, your chickens will sometimes need healthcare. Visits to the vet might be necessary, or you may need to buy medicine for illnesses like poultry bumblefoot, respiratory problems, and avian flu. Generally, poultry medicine for chickens is not expensive, and the diseases that spread through poultry are typically easy to manage. As a result, you should be able to rapidly gain control and medicate any illnesses that threaten your birds. Although a slight risk, the bird-to-human transmission of avian flu (H5N1) is still possible. H5N1 is a severe respiratory disease found in birds. It is highly infectious between birds. If a human catches H5N1, the mortality rate is approximately 60 percent. The good news is that backyard poultry farming produces a virtually zero chance of catching bird flu.

Wash your hands after handling chickens or touching their coop and other areas where they gather to minimize your risk of catching salmonella.

State Laws

You will need to check your local state law's regulations concerning keeping chickens. Your local city hall or zoning office will have ordinances that define how many birds you can keep, on how much land, and how close to roads, buildings, and so on. Regulations also tell you whether you need a permit and whether you are legally required to register your coop, apply for planning permission, and have it inspected. In addition, an ordinance will alert you on whether you are legally permitted to keep a rooster.

Do not give up hope if your local government does not permit you to raise backyard chickens. You can fill out paperwork and attend local government meetings to have the law changed in many areas. You will have a better chance of success if you work with other poultry enthusiasts in the area who would like to see the law changed too. Through the internet, you can easily find poultry lovers in your area with which to join forces.

Once you get permission, make sure to alert the neighbors of your plans. Assure them that you will be keeping a healthy, clean flock and will try your best not to cause too much noise with your chickens. You can always offer to bring delicious free-range eggs to gain your neighbor's goodwill and permission.

Predators

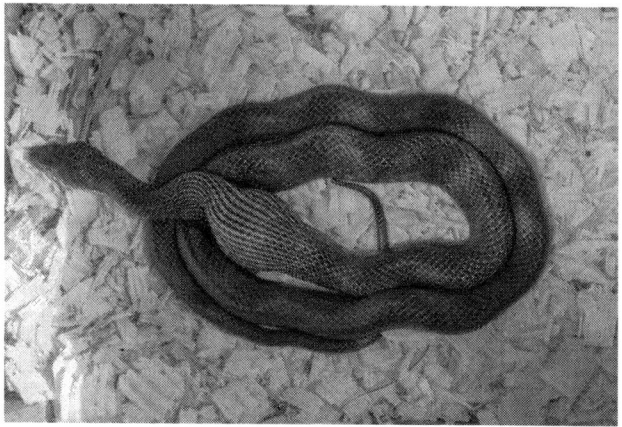

Your chicken is not just a potential source of food to you, but other wild animals in the area as well. If you live near predators like foxes, opossums, coyotes, skunks, weasels, or raccoons, you must bring your chickens in every night. Once predators find your flock, it becomes almost impossible to keep all of your chickens safe. Furthermore, your chickens could be in danger of daytime predators like neighboring cats and dogs. During pupping season, it is also important to be mindful of hawks, eagles, and sometimes even foxes. If you live in an area with a lot of predators, raising backyard chickens might not be the right decision.

Your birds' flightlessness is an evolutionary weakness. If predators are an issue and you still want to raise chickens, it will be necessary to create a secure enclosure for them during the day. You could also use a loyal pet, like a dog, to help guard your chickens.

Eggs

Chickens often lay eggs in their coop. At the same time, they will also lay eggs all over your backyard. This can become a problem if you cannot find their egg-laying spots. You will have to be watchful and clever to find these locations daily. If you do not, you may discover old eggs, only to mistake them for new eggs.

To fix this problem of what she terms "egg hunting", Elise (2017) said:

["When I first started free ranging chickens I felt like I was on a frustrating Easter Egg hunt every day! Once I learned their 'go to' laying spots, they changed it up on me again. (I once found over two dozen eggs nestled in some weeds under a tree in my pasture.)

Eventually I figured out how to outsmart my chickens.

I keep multiple highly desirable laying spots in my barn and keep a wooden or plastic egg in the nest. Because chickens have a natural instinct to want to clutch up eggs before they start sitting on a nest this method works for me most of the time.

Once in a while I do have a rogue chicken start laying somewhere funky (like in my goat's water trough) but this is a rare occurrence. I can remedy it most times by leaving a few eggs and in the nest to trigger those clutching instincts again.

Just make sure you mark those eggs with a sharpie so you do not accidentally eat them later. I assure you they will not be fresh."

Frequently Asked Questions

Q: Do my hens need roosters to lay eggs?

A: No. Roosters are not needed for your hens to lay eggs. Think about how a human woman can produce and release eggs without a human man. If you want to fertilize the eggs to create chicks, then you will need a rooster.

Q: How long will my chickens live?

A: Chickens have the same life expectancy as dogs: between eight and fifteen years. Even so, it is very rare for a chicken to live up to fifteen years.

Q: What supplies do I need to care for my new chicks?

A: Baby chicks need plenty of warmth in the first four weeks. Use a brooder with a single infrared lamp to keep the area at a constant ninety-five degrees fahrenheit. You might want to use an electronic thermometer to ensure that this temperature stays the same at all times.

Create a pen for your beautiful chicks using an eighteen-inch high corrugated paper chick corral. You can buy chick starter kits (minus infrared lamps and electronic thermometers) for as low as twenty dollars. Your chicks can roam outside in varying temperatures by weeks four and five.

Q: Does raising chickens save me money on food?

A: Raising chickens will not save you money, despite the opportunities to sell eggs, meat, and chicks. This is offset by the time and effort you must spend to raise and care for chickens. Furthermore, you must feed your chickens a well-balanced diet, make sure they have enough water, and keep them free of infections. At the most, you may break even since you no longer have to pay for free-range eggs and organic chicken from the supermarket.

Q: Where can I purchase chickens?

A: Chickens can cost as low as one dollar to as high as five dollars, although fancier breeds typically cost more. You can purchase chicks at a feed store or online.

Q: Do I need to wash my eggs?

A: You do not need to wash your eggs until you are just about to crack them. Each egg is laid with an invisible protective coating called "bloom" or "cuticle." Bloom prevents air and bacteria from entering the egg through the pores in the shell, preventing the egg from drying out from the inside. Gently rinse the eggs under warm running water before washing off the bloom.

Q: Do I need to refrigerate my eggs?

A: The bloom will also protect your eggs for several weeks so that they do not need to be refrigerated. Despite this, eggs typically last longer when refrigerated, so it might be best to refrigerate them if you do not plan to use them in a few days.

Q: How many eggs does a hen typically lay?

A: Hens do not lay eggs all year round. They are more active during the spring and summer months. During autumn, hens begin molting (losing their feathers and growing new ones for winter). Shorter days in autumn leave hens with a decreased level of sunlight. Since hens need fourteen hours of daylight to stimulate their ovaries, your hen may not lay another egg until spring. This autumn period gives your chicken's bodies a natural break from laying eggs before spring arrives again. You can bypass this seasonal change by installing a light in the coop. However, in doing so, you are placing a lot of stress on your hens' bodies.

Your breed of chicken also determines the number of eggs your hens lay. Some chickens lay an egg daily while others lay four to five weekly, approximately every other day. Expect that three hens will lay two eggs daily.

Hens have a limited time to lay eggs. They begin laying eggs at four to six months old, with their most fertile year being their first. It decreases after that, finally stopping by the end of the third year.

TWO

HOUSING AND CHICKEN COOP REQUIREMENTS

"You don't have to live on a farm to have chickens; in some places, you just need a little bit of green space and a tidy chicken coop. To me, they're nearly ideal pets. They feed us more often than we feed them! We have 2 chickens, Goldie and Paprika, and they each produce 1 egg a day, sometimes more."

-Amy Robach

BESIDES THE CHICKENS THEMSELVES, YOUR CHICKEN COOP is the most important purchase you need to make when raising chickens. Your coop is your chicken's home and place of rest, and if you do not have free-range chickens, the coop will be your chickens' permanent home. The coop is also where your chickens will lay most of their eggs; it is the center of your flock. For this reason, every decision you make concerning your coop must be made with utmost importance.

This chapter will teach you the major coop requirements you will need to meet as a beginner bird keeper. It will detail whether building your coop is better than buying a premade version, what bedding and accessories are required for your coop, and why. Finally, this chapter will include websites with plans to buy if you want to build your coop from scratch.

Why a Coop Is Important

A coop is your chickens' house. It protects them from bad weather, predators, injury, and theft. A coop is where your chickens can rest, safe from the threats of the outside world.

Your coop must be dry and draft-free. Build your coop in an area with good drainage to prevent water saturation and prolonged dampness of the floor of the enclosure and outside runs. You will also want a coop that has a second-floor nesting area. This is another barrier against water damage and additional protection for your chickens. Windows and doors are also essential so that you can ventilate your coop regularly.

When you have a greenhouse, you are encouraged to face the greenhouse to the south side for the best sun coverage. The same rules apply to a chicken coop. Face the front of the coop (the side with the most windows) on the south side. This will allow the sun to dry the enclosure and the soil inside while also warming it up. Your chickens will be grateful for this.

Your coop must be specifically designed to keep predators at bay. This is the coop's most crucial function because predators are generally a nuisance to both you and your chickens. Jennifer Poindexter (2021) wrote on her blog that:

> "Raccoons are wasteful creatures... I don't much care for them... I don't want you to eat any of my

livestock. However, if you are going to eat them... don't waste them!

Well, you will know a raccoon has been in your flock... if you find your birds dead with no head, but [the body is] not eaten. A lot of times raccoons will grab a chicken and try to drag it through the wire. Because chickens have small heads but big bodies, often all they can get is the head, so they'll eat that and leave. Raccoons like to go after chicks because they are an easy target."

Every coop needs a fence. Likewise, covered runs are your best protection from predators. If you are planning on building your coop, you can better protect your chickens by making it on a concrete floor. Start the wall with one or two concrete blocks to stop rodents, snakes, and other predators from digging under the walls and the floors. Securely cover windows and doors with heavy-gauge mesh wire or screening.

Predators will attempt to dig at the foundation of your coop fence. So, when building the outside runs, you must bury the wire along the pen border at least twelve inches deep, then toe (align) the fence outward about six inches. This is a necessity to stop most predators from digging under the fence. Indeed, when you align the fence outward and bury it, the predator is forced to dig down, only to meet more fencing. You may choose to run electric fencing around the outside of your chickens' pens four inches off the ground and about one foot from the main fence. This is a further incentive to avert predators.

If you do not take these protective measures for your outside runs, it will not be predator-proof. You will need to lock up your poultry before dark in that case.

Land predators are not your only worry. You must also reinforce your coop against attack from sky predators like hawks and owls. Do this by covering your outside runs with mesh wire or netting. You may also provide your birds with tall, leafy plants to hide under; consider tall and lush plants like sorghum, broomcorn, and millet. You may install a three to four-foot grid of baling twine over the pen for further protection.

Additionally, it would be best if you kept your flock locked in their coop when you are not around—unless you have a loyal dog that is happy to protect them. You may also use a burglar alarm within the vicinities of your coop or ask a neighbor to periodically check that everything is fine.

Do not get carried away with protective measures. Remember, they are to keep predators out, not lock your chickens inside. Ensure that they are not designed in such a way to hurt your birds. Inspect the area regularly for loose wire, nails, or any other sharp-edged objects that may have come off the structure, like a jagged piece of wood. Since chickens can only fly a few inches off the ground for a few seconds, you will want to keep them as close to the ground as possible. Take precautions to remove any areas (other than perches) that are more than four feet above the ground. Your chicken could attempt to perch there, only to face injury or death when trying to jump back down. To prevent this, you will want to remove these potential perching areas, such as window sills, electric cords, and loose crates.

Nesting Boxes: Their Role and Importance

Consider the nesting box as your chicken's living room and bedroom furniture. It is there to make your chickens' experience a pleasant and enjoyable one. Hens love sitting on nesting boxes for comfortable, quiet seats, especially when laying eggs. You will find that your hens will typically sit and lay their eggs in private. Once their eggs are laid, the hens are no longer interested in this quiet, comfortable seat and will ignore it until the next time they need to lay eggs.

In a personal example given in the previous chapter, Elise complained about her chickens leaving eggs in hidden places all over her pasture. Chickens have survived many years by finding safe and quiet spots in nature to build their nest. Therefore, the nesting boxes are really for you, the keeper.

You want to find the eggs as quickly as possible without conducting an intensive egg hunt every day. You may leave the nesting boxes in your yard, but this is ill-advised because of predators. I keep my nests in the well-protected coop so my hens feel safe and relaxed enough to produce their eggs.

Hens like variety, so if you have space, place the nesting boxes at different locations in the coop. Your hen can choose which she would like to use to lay her egg for the day. I make sure to place my nesting boxes away from the feeding station and away from the undersides of perches. Remember that your hen needs quiet to lay her eggs, and the perch and the feeding station are both far from quiet. Your hen would prefer for her nesting box to be in a darkened area of the coop. She needs meditation and peace to lay her egg.

Always place your nesting box raised from the floor by eighteen to twenty-four inches. Additionally, the roosts must always be higher than the nest boxes to discourage the hens from sleeping in the boxes. Use at least one 1 foot x 1 foot nest box for every four or five hens in the flock, and never use fewer than six nesting boxes.

Fundamentals Of Nesting Boxes

You will need one nesting box per three to four chickens. If you have more than ten chickens or so under the age of three, then change this to one nesting box per two to three chickens. This ensures that every hen will have a nesting box whenever needed.

Be aware that hens pick favorite nesting boxes, which could eventually lead to altercations between your chickens. Everything you build for your chickens should be based on their personality. Since chickens love variety, you can even add a couple of nesting boxes outside the coop for whichever hen you have who may play by her own rules. Simply keep your eyes peeled for predators whenever you are at home, and leave your hens locked in the coop when you are not.

Each nesting box should be individual-sized, meaning that it can only fit one hen. If you have more than one hen laying an egg in the same box, the eggs could break. Choose the size of your nesting boxes based on the size of chickens that you have:

- Standard sized chickens: 12-inch x 12 inch x 12-inch boxes

- Bantams chickens: 10 inch x 12 inch x 10 inch boxes

- Larger breeds, like Jersey Giants: 12-inch x 14-inch x 12-inch boxes

For best results, choose a nesting box made of wood or plastic. They are durable, and you can wash them every time you clean the coop. I use wood because it is the better of the two. It can be built to be sturdy and to last a long time.

Finally, you must consider the issue of safety by attaching your box to the inside of your coop. Most nesting boxes that you can buy premade will attach to the wall of your coop. Pre-built boxes even come with pre-drilled holes to allow you to easily screw them to the wall of the coop. Therefore, you must make sure that the framework of your coop can support the number of boxes you intend to place inside. Wooden boxes are significantly heavier than plastic boxes and will need extra support to be held in place. If you decide to use wooden nesting boxes, you may need to build a more robust and bigger coop that can withstand heavier weights.

So You Want to Build a Coop?

If you prefer to use a hand-built coop over a store-bought, premade one, there are a few things to consider.

They Can Be Expensive

Hand-built coops last longer but are more expensive. The cost is worth it because you can build a coop according to your needs and specifications. Similarly, try asking local box stores or other companies if they have any pallets they want to get rid of. I built my nest boxes by visiting a local construction site near my house and asking them for waste pallets. This brought some of my costs down. If you already have a treehouse or doghouse that you no longer use, this can be easily transformed into a coop.

They Need Enough Space

Your chickens need space. They feel overcrowded otherwise, so it is best to build a spacious coop. Ensure that your coop is built with outside runs (the open ground surrounded by netting where chickens roam). In the outdoor runs, your chicken can exercise and roam happily. Some coops don't have outside runs and have to compensate with an even bigger space inside the coop.

Your hens will move, exercise, nest, and rest in the coop. The amount of space you need inside the coop depends on the type of chickens you keep. Bantam chickens, for example, require two square feet per bird inside the coop and four square feet per bird in the outside runs. On the other hand, large chickens need two to three square feet per bird inside the enclosure and ten square feet per bird in the outdoor runs. Do not be afraid to make your coop larger if you have space. The more room your flock has, the happier they will be. You'll also need to provide six to ten inches of perch space per chicken.

Avoid overcrowding your chickens at all costs. It will cause your chickens to fight more, leaving the weaker chickens unable to access enough food and water. The chickens at the bottom of the pecking order could even show cuts and wounds from being pecked at by the other chickens. Additionally, fecal matter builds up quickly in an overcrowded coop. This brings in bacteria and parasites, which can harm your chickens.

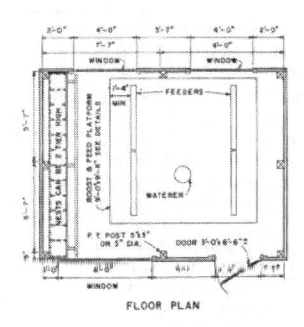

FLOOR PLAN

Above is an example of a coop's space plan designed by Virginia State University (Clauer, 2021).

. . .

They Need Easy Access to Feed and Water

Your coop will need easy access to feed and water. To do so, place feeders and waterers in convenient locations throughout the pen. To keep the feed and water clean, place the waterers and the feeders at chicken height, and make sure you use waterers and feeders with the least amount of wastage and spill. Your chickens will need two to three linear inches of water and feed space per bird.

If you can, place your waterer in the outside runs of the coop. If you put it inside, the humidity level inside the coop will increase. Increased humidity levels will cause health problems for your chickens.

Below is an example of a coop's feed and water plan, designed by Virginia State University (Clauer, 2021).

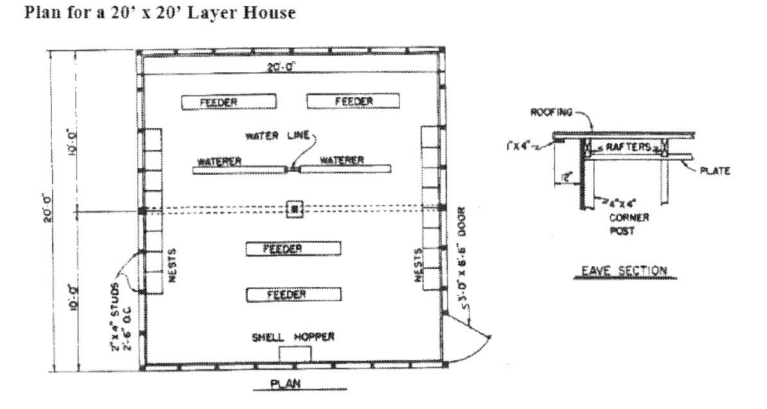

Plan for a 20' x 20' Layer House

They Need Ventilation

You will need to keep your coop well-ventilated but not drafty. Fresh air brings in oxygen and blows out excess moisture, carbon dioxide, and ammonia. If your enclosure is not well-ventilated, it will become damp and show ammonia build-up. Your coop will also need to be well-insulated, with a good vapor barrier. Without proper insulation or ventilation, the walls and ceilings will begin to hold moisture in cool weather. This may cause many health problems for your chickens in cold weather. Chickens can survive well in cold weather, as long as they are dry. You must check that the coop's opening is on the southern or eastern side of the coop, facing away from prevailing winds.

Below is an example of a coop's plan, including a south-facing door, windows, and a vent, as designed by Virginia State University (Clauer, 2021).

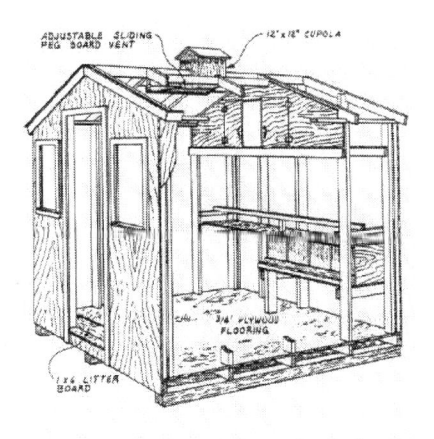

Plywood Is the Best Material

Plywood is the best material for building your coop because it is relatively cheap and highly durable, as long as you protect it with primer and paint. It is also effortless to build with since you can easily cut holes and windows through it. You can use unfinished plywood for the flooring. Simply add a deep layer of shavings. To make it easier to clean, you may roll down a layer of linoleum on top, as linoleum is easy to clean and replace if needed. Some people also prefer concrete floors, as discussed earlier.

Here is an example of a coop made out of plywood, as designed by Virginia State University (Clauer, 2021).

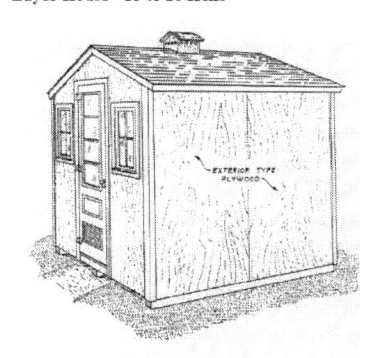

Plan for an 8' x 8' Layer House - 15 to 20 Hens

They Need Electricity

As discussed previously, hens stop producing eggs in colder months because they do not receive enough light. If you want eggs in colder months, your coop will need electric light. For a small chicken coop measuring about one hundred square feet

(10 foot x 10 foot), a 40-watt bulb is enough to extend daylight for a few hours in the early morning. Do not extend it during the night because you will confuse your hens if the light goes out at night, revealing nothing but darkness.

Always keep the bulb about seven feet from the coop's floor. If you have a bigger coop, measuring upwards of two hundred square feet (20 foot x 20 foot), a 60-watt bulb is sufficient. Your hens still need to rest, so you will need a timer to keep the lights on for no more than fourteen hours a day. Do not begin using the bulb in winter. If you do, you will disorient your hens by suddenly reducing their nighttime hours. Begin in late summer, adding forty-five minutes every week to compensate for shorter daylight hours.

Use one electric light on the ceiling for every forty square feet. If you have a small coop, one light above the feeding and watering area is more than enough to do the job.

Placing windows on the southern side of the coop is also a good source of light and warmth for your birds.

They Need a Good Location

The location of your coop is critical, as discussed in this chapter. Exposure to sunlight and warmth from the south is essential. You must also consider any nearby structures to which you may wish to attach your coop. Finally, your coop must be elevated above the ground if you want to avoid mud and water problems.

. . .

They Should Be Well-Built

This chapter provides you with examples of coop designs that you can use. Designing your structure is very important. Without a well-designed layout, your coop may not be as efficient as it should be. Make sure that your nests, rafters, and feeders are easily accessible at all times. While building my coop, I sloped the floor slightly to prevent water from building up. This also made my coop floor easier to dry. I also secured my coop door and windows well using spring-loaded eye-hooks and latches secured with carabiners or padlocks. If I did not secure my coop like this, some predators, like raccoons, would be able to turn its knobs and lift its latches.

You also want your coop to be as visibly well-constructed as possible to appeal to your neighbors. Keep the exterior well-designed, well-painted, and the surrounding area well-kept and neat. This means that you will not want any weeds or trash lying around. You will also want to be considerate of your neighbors while designing your coop; insulate the inside to muffle the day-to-day sounds of your chickens. Your neighbors will not be happy if they hear noisy chickens all day. Suppose your coop is not well-groomed, nice to look at, and considerately designed. In that case, your neighbors may complain to the local council, who may enact new laws restricting your ability to raise backyard chickens.

Buying a Premade Coop

If you choose a premade coop, you can purchase them from reputable sources. These include: Wayfair.com, Tractorsupply.com, Amazon.com, Overstock.com, and Mypetchicken.com.

These stores sell a variety of coops to meet different needs. You can buy wire meshes only or coops with outside runs. They also come in different sizes and shapes, and some will come with nesting boxes. You may even buy moveable ones and attachable ones. However, some coops are not raised off the ground. It is best not to purchase these because they do not protect against mud or water damage.

Building from Scratch

You will need the required tools to get started on building your coop. You will also need the parts for making a coop. Before you begin purchasing materials or tools, you will first need to decide what coop plan to follow. Many websites offer coop plans, such as Etsy.com, Mypetchicken.com, and Amazon.com.

You can also find free chicken coop plans on the internet. Texas A&M Agrilife Extension offers free, innovative, and creative chicken coop ideas. For example, did you know that you can reuse old car frames, old dollhouses, and trampolines as chicken coops? You can also find very creative chicken coop ideas at Backyardchickens.com, including a spaceship coop and a camper van coop. Your neighbors will surely appreciate seeing such innovative enclosures in your backyard.

Required Equipment

- **Personal Safety Gear:** You will need work gloves, protective eye goggles, and hearing protection. These are the most critical items in your toolkit.

- **Tin Snips:** Tin snips help you cut through wire mesh and other tough materials, like baling twine.

- **Speed Square:** A speed square helps you mark straight lines and angles for cutting.

- **Tape Measure:** You will need a ten–fifteen-foot long tape measure.

- **Hammer:** You will need a hammer that you can swing with ease. You will use the hammer to knock in nails and knock wood into position. If you are building a large coop, use a pneumatic nailer.

- **Circular Saw:** You will need it to cut through wood to various sizes. You may also need to use a miter saw, a table saw, a jigsaw, and a handsaw for more detail-oriented tasks.

- **Drill:** This is perfect for twisting in screws.

- **Level (You'll need different types of levels for the job):**

- A pocket-sized torpedo level

- A medium, two-foot model level

- A long, four-foot carpenter's level

Basic Requirements For A Coop

- **Nest Box:** The importance of nest boxes is discussed in Chapter One. Try to have more nest boxes than you need to prevent overcrowding your chickens.

- **Waterer:** Water is the most critical element in a

chicken's diet. You must ensure that your flock has clean, fresh water at all times. This helps you avoid growth and egg production issues and keeps your birds healthy. You can buy waterers in an assortment of designs.

- **Roosting Bars:** Most chicken breeds prefer to roost or perch to sleep at night. A roosting bar makes your chicken more comfortable throughout the night. Add at least one bar per bird (or a bar long enough for multiple birds to perch on). You will also want to smooth off the edges on the bars' top surfaces. This minimizes potential foot discomfort.

- **Feeder:** Food is another vital ingredient for healthy

chickens. They come in various designs, such as hanging feeders that are to be suspended from the coop ceiling and bucket feeders that can store a few days' worth of feed. Floor feeders must have a lip deep enough to stop too much feed from spilling onto the coop floor.

- **Waterer Upgrade:** A waterer upgrade with a heated base will keep the water in the coop from freezing on cold days and nights. Use a continuous-flow design to keep the water from becoming stagnant.

- **Thermometer And Heater:** You will need brooder thermometers and a heating element to hatch and raise chicks. You need a heating element, such as a heat lamp, because chicks cannot produce enough energy to keep themselves warm. A brooder thermometer monitors the chicks' habitat's actual temperature, increasing or decreasing the heat when needed.

- **Electric Fencing:** Keep your free-range flock safe from predators inside electric fencing. Add electric fencing using a simple one- or two-wire system or electrified poultry netting or hot wires added to existing fencing.

- **Wheels:** If your coop is not too large, you can attach wheels to the frame to move it around the yard. This is a good practice for fertilizing your backyard. When chickens scratch and pick at the soil, searching for bugs and plant material, they aerate the ground under their feet. When they leave droppings on the aerated ground, it fertilizes the soil.

- **Edible Plants:** I supplement my chickens' diet with edible plants, like spinach, lettuce, watermelon, and comfrey. This varies their diet, providing them with more sources of nutrients. Do not let your chickens eat grass because grass clippings are hard to digest for chickens. This may cause impaction. Furthermore, people often treat grass with herbicides and insecticides, which can impact your chickens' health.

- **Toys:** I love to provide my hens with shiny, edible toys. Toys generally distract chickens from fighting by keeping them entertained. Once in a while, I give my chickens edible toys by making or buying an edible block treat. Block treats contain various grains, meals, and grits. It is like a delicious puzzle for my chickens to keep them entertained and healthy. They slowly break apart the block, seeking more treats. At the same time, they exercise their natural scratching and pecking instincts. Visit Chapter Four for an excellent block treat recipe.

- **Security Motion Sensor Lights:** Security motion sensor lights will keep your chickens safe from predators at night. They will alert you to the presence of predators and scare off any predators who want to use the cover of night to steal some chickens.

- **Security And Access Door:** An automatic chicken door will ensure that your coop door is always closed at night. If you use one with GPS technology, you can keep your coop door closed even when you are away.

- **Solar-Powered Light:** You can use a solar-operated chicken coop light instead of electric lights. A solar-operated light keeps your hens warm and provides them with the right amount of sunlight so that their egg-laying schedule isn't interrupted by the colder months. Furthermore, you can easily install one.

It costs nothing once it is installed, unlike an electric light.

Chicken Tractors

A chicken tractor is a portable chicken coop. It contains everything your chicken needs in her house. It includes food, water, a roosting perch, and a nesting box to keep your chicken happy. At the same time, it allows your hen to free-range.

The tractor keeps your chickens inside the coop, so they don't damage the rest of your yard. It's also mobile so that you can move your chickens to different patches of grass. This will allow the previous patch of grass to recover while the chickens fertilize another area of your yard. Your hens will also eat the weeds and insects in your yard, keeping it neat and tidy. Make sure you move the tractor every other day to avoid creating bald spots or a dust bath crater in your yard.

The tractor also keeps your hens safe from predators, especially aerial predators like hawks and owls. An excellent sturdy tractor keeps out most predators. However, chicken tractors occasionally are unable to keep out bears, coyotes, and raccoons.

Tips for Building a Successful Coop

- Choose wisely whether you want your chickens to be free-range or confined.

- Confinement promotes contagious diseases like coccidiosis, but a free-range lifestyle attracts the attention of predators.

- Keep your coop clean and well-ventilated but draft-free. Your waterer and feeder must always be kept clean, too.

- Use good bedding, such as sawdust (untreated wood only), chopped straw, or wood shavings.

- Do not overcrowd your coop. This causes the stronger hens to pick on the weaker hens and makes disease spread faster.

- Do not construct your coop in a hurry. It is better to be well-prepared and build a good, long-lasting coop than rush through and build a poor-quality one. It would help if you had solid plans and sketches that meet all requirements and have all of your tools ready. Ensure you have thought about all the variables involved in building a coop, such as; size, cost, portability, and maintenance plans.

- Make sure that your coop is functional. For example, its doors must open inwards, not outwards. If they open outwards, your hens might try to run out.

- Make sure that you use high-quality material that will last a long time.

- Make it easy to clean and maintain. Add a human-sized door in the plans so you can easily enter to clean it out.

- Make your coop safe from predators by building predator-proof fences, such as electric fences.

Bedding Materials

The correct bedding material will keep your chickens healthy and prevent their eggs from cracking. Good litter provides a secure, soft landing for your chicken's eggs, legs, and feet. You can gather chicken droppings quickly and easily clean your coop with sufficient bedding.

Deep clean and disinfect your chicken coop once a year to avoid illnesses for your chickens. Chicken litter typically lasts six months before you need to change it. It stays that long because chicken droppings become incorporated into the shavings as the chickens stir them. Every six months, you should scoop the old litter using a shovel or a snow shovel and replace it with fresh bedding.

The myth that chickens smell bad is untrue. You can avoid odors by changing your coop's bedding regularly. Chickens only stink when they're crammed into enclosures without fresh air and ventilation or when their bedding gets wet. The best types of beddings absorb plenty of moisture, insulate the floor to keep the coop warm and give chickens a chance to dust.

Bedding materials that create a little dust are also perfect for chicken coops because chickens love to dust themselves. They fluff litter into their feathers regularly for dust baths (see Chapter Seven), killing parasites in the process. Always use sand or dirt as an undercoating for your bedding.

Shavings and straw are the two most popular beddings. Still, there are a variety of bedding materials to choose from, including:

. . .

Straw/Hay

Straw smells sweet and earthy, covering up bad smells from chicken droppings. It has a springy texture that keeps freshly laid eggs safe and protected. It is cheap but not nearly as absorbent as wood chips. Furthermore, it tends to become matted down, making it harder to shovel out than wood chips.

Pine Shavings

Pine shavings are very popular because they are affordable and widespread. You can find them at many feed stores, big-box stores, and even pet supply stores. They are an ideal bedding material because they dry fast and don't break down quickly. The mild pine scent masks the smell of chicken droppings, although it does fade over time.

Wood Shavings

Chickens do not urinate. They expel all their waste through their droppings. This makes wood shavings very useful in coops, and they are the most commonly used litter. Four to six inches of dry wood shavings will last you six months or more. You can buy them from most big-box stores and wood supply stores. You may even ask woodworkers if they have any spare wood shavings to give you. Wood shavings smell pleasant and are amazingly absorbent. They also don't pack down, making them the best bedding for nesting boxes. You can mix in some crushed and dried herbs, like mint or lavender, to keep away pests. These aromatic oils typically don't have any adverse effects on your chickens.

I prefer to compost used wood shavings every six months. I work a thin layer into garden soil to provide nutrients and water absorbency for my ground and plants.

However, suppose your wood shavings get wet. In that case, typically because a waterer leaked or tipped over, you must change it immediately to prevent odors from forming. When litter gets wet (usually when a waterer leaks or tips over), I immediately remove the soggy shavings and replace them with fresh dry ones.

Avoid redwood and cedar shavings because they carry toxins that can cause breathing and eye issues for your poultry.

Sawdust

Sawdust works well as bedding, but it's too dusty for chickens. Chickens stir it up, and the dust settles on everything in the coop. Sawdust is also known for causing respiratory issues in chickens.

Dried Leaves

Dried leaves make a suitable chicken litter. Unfortunately, they're only available in the fall, and they tend to break down into dust very quickly. You can also use shredded leaves. You will have to finely shred the leaves so that they can dry quickly. Unshredded, whole leaves take too long to break down and harbor moisture, causing them to stick together and matt. If leaf bedding gets wet, it becomes slippery, leading to splayed legs or bumblefoot, especially in younger, growing birds.

Sand

Sand is an excellent and very clean bedding choice. It does not break down, it dries fast, and it is an ideal material for dust baths (see Chapter Seven). However, it is expensive and time-consuming. You can use sand for the inside of your coop and the floor of your outside runs. Make sure you use builder's sand because sandbox sand is too fine and clumps. You can easily find builder's sand in home-improvement stores.

Recycled Paper

Shredded newspapers, books, magazines, flyers, and paper can be used as bedding. Although free, the ink can be toxic to chickens. Office paper is also heavily processed and treated. Glossy paper from magazines and fliers also contains a large amount of ink, creating a matted, slippery surface for your chickens.

Grass Clippings

If you have a lot of grass in your yard, you can use grass clippings. However, be aware that grass clippings retain moisture and break down quickly. This causes them to dry out, shrink and stink. You must use organic grass. If you opt for non-organic grass clippings, your chickens may ingest the pesticides, fungicides, herbicides, or other chemicals used on the grass.

The Deep-Litter Method

Most backyard chicken owners use the "deep litter" method because it is easy and sustainable. This method creates a compost pile from the poop on the bottom of the coop.

The deep-litter method is very popular because it does not require much time or effort. It involves building layered bedding starting with a layer of organic matter like wood shavings. This organic matter forms the "browns," or the brown matter used for composting—the chicken droppings from the high-nitrogen "greens" needed for compost. You will need to turn the bedding over every week and add a new layer.

This method works by breaking down and decomposing the older bedding and chicken waste in the coop while providing natural warmth for your chickens. By the second month, you will have created deep litter, and by the twelfth month, you will have fully built-up compost. Once the bedding grows, it tends to trickle out as your chickens come and go. Use a plywood board at the coop door to prevent the chickens from trailing the litter outside of the coop.

Dropping Boards

You can save money using a dropping board (if you're not using the deep-litter method). Chickens release the most waste at night. You can place a dropping board or tray on the floor to catch any droppings before they reach the bedding. This prevents large quantities of excrement from landing on your shavings, leaving your coop dry and clean. You can easily clean up the waste on the dropping board in the mornings, saving you time and effort. A dropping board is also a good long-term way of saving money because you won't need to clean out your shavings as frequently.

Cleaning Your Coop

You must deep-clean your coop once a year to remove mold, parasites, and mildew. Spring is a great time to deep-clean your coop. You will want to remove everything inside the enclosure to deep-clean. This way, you will have space to clean your coop from top to bottom, shoveling and replacing bedding, sweeping, vacuuming, and washing.

To clean my coop, I place a few nesting boxes outside to sit my hens. Then I lock the coop door so that they cannot get back in. As a very deep clean may take all day, I clear my schedule and prepare accordingly. It is a big job, and I always get at least some help.

This is how I clean my coop:

1. First I remove all the nesting boxes and place them outside the enclosure.
2. I shovel the deep-litter bedding into the compost pile.
3. Then I sweep the coop and remove cobwebs from window sills and shelves.
4. I vacuum the entire coop.
5. I power-wash the entire coop to remove stubborn, built-in stains.
6. I use a shovel to hand scrape all of the leftover dried poop on the floor. I need to scrape out as much of the bird droppings as I can since they will not soften with the help of water or a cleansing solution.
7. Next I use a hose to spray down the floor and the walls, cleaning dust and debris.
8. I soak the floor and walls with a bucket of sudsy water treated with a half bottle of hydrogen peroxide. I spread the water around with a broom and brush to ensure that the soapy water gets over the floor and walls.
9. I use a natural cleaning agent and disinfectant, like vinegar. I never use bleach because it is too harsh for animals to bear. It can also be toxic to my hens if they

are let back into the coop before it is completely dried.
10. Then I rinse the whole coop until all the cleaning product comes off. If the smell lingers, I repeat the soap-water process. It is essential to scrub out the odor in the coop, even if it will return in a few days.
11. I scrub down the nesting boxes, waterers, lights, feeders, and other items in the coop.
12. Next I allow the coop to air dry until everything is completely dry.
13. Once the coop and its equipment have dried, I arrange everything back inside.
14. I place two bales of new wood shavings or straw on the floor.
15. I return the washed nesting boxes to their shelves and let my hens go back into the coop.
16. Finally, I wash and air dry the nesting boxes that the chicken sat on while I cleaned the coop.

THREE

SELECTING THE RIGHT BREED

"I haven't checked, but I highly suspect that chickens evolved from an egg-laying ancestor, which would mean that there were, in fact, eggs before there were chickens. Genius."

-Ta-Nehisi Coates

THERE IS A VARIETY OF ROOSTER AND HEN BREEDS YOU CAN raise in your backyard. You will have to choose your species depending on their qualities. For example, if you want calm, quiet, and friendly chickens, you can purchase Brahma hens. If you prefer more outgoing chickens, you may choose Buckeye hens.

Hen Breeds

Bantam Hens

Bantams are mini-breeds that come in all chicken varieties. They are usually just one-quarter to one-half of the regular size of their breed. Since they are not too big, they make excellent chickens for residential neighborhoods.

Australorp Hens

Australorps are Australian Black Orpingtons. They can grow up to six pounds as adults. They are typically black, but they can be blue or white too. However, only the black variety is recognized in the United States.

Pros

- Charming, friendly, and gentle, making them extraordinary beginner chickens. While they are shy at first, they become very friendly once they get used to you.

- Get along well with other chickens and other animals.

- Bred specifically to produce eggs and can lay over 300 large brown eggs a year (although, on average, they lay about 250 eggs).

- Good nest sitters and good mothers to their chicks.

- Thrive as backyard birds and are easy to take care of.

Cons

- Need access to shade during all hours of the day.

- While they tolerate the heat very well, they are the breed of chickens most susceptible to strokes.

- Like to roam around and be active as opposed to being entirely confined.

- Prone to obesity if kept in confinement.

Brahma Hens

Brahmas are named after the Brahmaputra River that runs through India, Tibet, and Bangladesh. They originate from Chittagong fowl from India.

Brahmas are also known as the "King of Chickens" because of their large size. Hens can reach anywhere from seven to nine pounds, and Bantams can get thirty-two to thirty–eight ounces. Their varieties include Light, Dark, and Buff.

Pros

- Very friendly and love the company of humans; just make sure they are raised in the company of humans as chicks. They enjoy taking treats from human hands.

- Quiet, gentle, and calm birds who get along well with other chickens.

- Fluffy feathers, legs, and feet that help them survive colder months.

- Make perfect pets and are happy when kept behind a two-foot fence.

- Lay about 150 eggs per year.

Cons

- Produce most of their eggs from October through May, meaning that they will not have eggs for about four months of the year. If you want hens that can produce eggs all year round, do not only choose Brahmas.

Barnevelder Hens

Barnevelders, or "Barneys," were made by crossing Dutch chickens with breeds from Asia. Double-laced Barnevelders are the only Barnevelder variety recognized by the American Poultry Association. In the United States, you can find blue double-laced varieties, although they are not recognized as a standard.

Pros

- Stunning to look at, with distinct markings on their

feathers. (Roosters do not have this distinctive pattern on their feathers.)

- Easy-going, quiet, and peaceful. They make great pets if you train them from a young age.

- Enjoy the company of humans and love to be around children.

- Naturally lay eggs through the winter.

- Active birds that like to be kept free-range.

- Lay about 150 dark brown eggs per year.

Cons

- Love to chat, but their voices are low and quiet.

Dorking Hens

Dorkings are one of the oldest known chicken breeds. However, they're currently endangered because commercial chicken farmers prefer faster-growing chicken breeds. Dorkings are also a few breeds of chickens with a fifth toe, although this toe has no use.

Pros

- Meat is known as one of the best-tasting varieties of chicken meat.

- Lay about 150–200 medium to large eggs annually.

- Naturally produce eggs throughout the year.

- Love to be kept free-range and will forage your property for bugs and weeds.

Cons

- Too sweet and docile and tend to end up at the bottom of the pecking order.

- Due to their shorter legs, Dorking hens get dirtier and

messier much quicker than other hens. You will need to give them unscheduled baths as a result.

- Grow slower and mature slower than other hens.

Golden Comet Hens

Golden Comet hens are one of the most popular backyard chickens. They were initially bred for commercial egg production and weigh about four pounds.

Pros

- Can produce almost one egg per day, averaging around 300 eggs per year.

- Typically start laying eggs at sixteen weeks old and stop at the end of their second or third year.

- Love human companionship, sometimes over other chickens. They even like being picked up and petted.

- Very friendly and gentle.

- Curious and often get into funny situations.

- Very hardy and can tolerate a wide variety of temperatures.

- Do not like squabbling or pecking. They prefer peace.

- Quiet and take up little space, making them ideal for a small backyard.

Cons

- Will need to be replaced with younger hens after they stop producing eggs by the second to third year.

- Rarely brood. If you want chicks, you will need an incubator.

- Need to keep them with other docile breeds, like the Dorking; otherwise, they will be bullied.

- Do not breed Golden Comet chicks. To get a Golden

comet chick, you will need to crossbreed a New Hampshire rooster with a White Rock hen.

- Live for four to five years.

- Often suffer from illnesses related to their egg production, like egg yolk peritonitis and other reproductive tumors.

Jersey Giant Hens

Jersey Giants are the largest purebred chickens in the United States and one of the largest in the world. They're almost as big as Brahmas. They were bred to produce plenty of meat for roasting. Still, they were immediately overshadowed by the introduction of the giant turkey.

They are a rare breed in the United States because they are not used in industrial poultry farming. Jersey Giant Hens can grow to a height of sixteen–twenty inches and weigh up to eleven pounds.

Pros

- Gentle, friendly chickens that make great pets. They also really like children.

- Lay 150–200 large eggs yearly.

- Love foraging and moving around to develop their muscles. They do not like being confined.

- Have very delicious meat that can feed a family of four.

- A very healthy breed.

Cons

- Mature very slowly.

- Usually do not go broody and are often so big, breaking their eggs. You will need an incubator if you want to raise Jersey Giant chicks. Alternatively, you can place their eggs under another breed of chicken. (See the end of this chapter for a detailed explanation of broody hens.)

- Need a big coop, with a minimum of four square feet per bird for Jersey Giant hens.

- Need more backyard space because of their size.

- Can quickly develop bone and muscle weakness. You must give them vitamins regularly to avoid this.

- Cost more in feed because they eat more and take longer to mature.

- Prone to developing infections and bumblefoot from landing their heavy bodies on sharp objects. You will have to check their feet regularly to catch any problems. Treating problems will keep your Jersey Giant Hens healthy.

New Hampshire Hens

The New Hampshire is a hardy chicken that looks similar to the Rhode Island Red. The hens can reach about six pounds, with Bantam hens reaching thirty ounces.

Pros

- Healthy chickens with no significant health problems.

- Easy to tame and family-friendly. They are also intelligent and reliable chickens.

- Go broody often and make great mothers if they hatch their eggs. Some have been seen accepting other chicks as their own.

- Foragers who like to roam rather than being confined.

Cons

- Some New Hampshire hens can be unfriendly and aggressive, especially with food. They sometimes push more docile chickens out of the way. It is best not to keep them with more gentle chickens.

- Need shady spots in the heat.

Plymouth Rock Hens

This is America's oldest chicken breed. It was the country's primary source of chicken and eggs until the end of World War II. But they lost popularity once industrialized farming took over because they did not produce enough eggs and meat. They are known for their distinct barred black and white feathers, although there are other varieties.

Pros

- A good source of meat and eggs, laying about 200 eggs a year.

- Remarkably gentle birds that get along with other chickens and people. They do not peck other chickens, and they are friendly to families and children.

- Lay fewer eggs by the third year, but some Plymouth Rock hens have been known to lay eggs well into their tenth year.

- Mature very quickly between weeks eight and twelve.

- Very curious and will follow you around the backyard.

- Only need a small fence to keep them in because they can barely lift themselves off the ground.

- Their breed has no particular health problems.

- Typically live for ten to twelve years. Some of them have lived for twenty years. They live longer if you take excellent care of them.

- Love attention and cuddles. They can quickly become lap chickens.

- Are a breeze to care for and easy-going.

Cons

- Need plenty of space when confined. They prefer to be free-range and forage for their food.

- Talkative, although quiet.

Rhode Island Red Hens

The Rhode Island Red hen can weigh up to six and a half pounds. Bantam Rhode Island Reds are rare and can weigh up to two pounds.

Pros

- One of the best egg-laying breeds. They can lay between 200 and 300 eggs a year, laying five to six medium to large eggs a week. The eggs are brown and increase in size as the hen grows older.

- Love to forage and free-range.

- Vary in temperament but are generally friendly, laid back, and docile. They can be curious and pushy.

- Enjoy the company of people, especially children.

- Will eat larger pests in your yard, like frogs and mice.

- A very healthy and active breed with no known health problems.

- A very hardy breed that can survive in poor conditions. They can also survive most climates.

- Watchful for predators and are quick to attack threats.

Cons

- Make a lot of noise.

- Rarely get broody but are very protective when they do.

- Tolerate confinement but prefer to forage.

- Prefer to lay their eggs around the yard and often ignore nesting boxes. You will need to search for eggs around the yard daily and watch out not to accidentally eat eggs that are not fresh.

White Rock Hens

The White Rock chicken is a variety of the Plymouth Rock chicken. They come in many colors, but the white varieties are the most popular. They are known as the "traditional" American farm chickens because they are so versatile, producing plenty of meat and eggs. They are standard-size chickens, weighing around eight pounds.—the perfect size for a family roast.

Pros

- The best variety for egg-laying (along with the Rhode Island Red), laying an egg per day if cared for correctly.

- Produce eggs throughout the winter if they are healthy and well-tended.

- Survive well in colder climates because of their fluffy feathers.

- Prefer to forage for their daily protein needs. They only use feeders when they are tired from foraging.

- Very intelligent and skilled at watching out for predators.

- Very docile and friendly.

- Do not often go broody but are very protective of their chicks if left to raise them independently.

Cons

- Prone to frostbite because of the single comb on their head. You will have to apply Vaseline on their comb and insulate their coop well to prevent frostbite.

- Their color means they are at greater risk of being spotted by predators and have more significant problems camouflaging themselves, unlike other breeds.

- Very docile and friendly, but this leaves them easy targets for more assertive hens.

Rooster Breeds

Brahma Roosters

Brahmas are also known as the "King of Chickens" because of their large size. Roosters can reach ten pounds. Bantam Brahmas weigh between thirty-four and thirty-eight ounces.

They were brought to the United States by sailors returning from Shanghai, China. They can be light, dark, buff, black and white, although the black and white ones are rare.

Pros

- Big, feathery birds that look intimidating, especially to children. However, they are very gentle and friendly.

- Easy to handle and very calm.

- Do not fly well, so they are easily contained.

- Tolerate confinement well, but they prefer to forage.

- Their heavily feathered feet make them survive cold climates well.

- Very healthy birds with no significant health problems.

- May show more dominance in the spring but are generally docile, loving pets.

Cons

- Eat more than regular roosters.

- Require a bigger coop, door, and coop furniture to accommodate your roosters.

- Brahma roosters do not do well in wet, swampy, or muddy areas because of their feathered feet. Their feathers can become damp and dirty, leading to frostbite during freezing temperatures.

- Feathers are dense and tight, so you will need to keep an eye out for lice and mites. As a feathered-foot breed, you will also need to inspect their legs regularly for scaly leg mites. Be very thorough—it is challenging to spot scaly leg mites in feather-foot breeds.

- Sometimes foot quills (the shaft of a feather) catch on to objects and break off. This can cause your chicken to bleed quite profusely. You will have to apply pressure to the area, then add cornstarch or styptic powder.

Buff Orpington Roosters

Orpington chicken breeds were considered endangered until 2016. Since then, the breed was removed from the American Breed Livestock Conservancy list because backyard chicken keepers bred them back from endangerment.

. . .

A Buff Orpington rooster will typically weigh ten pounds. A Bantam will weigh about thirty-eight ounces and is one of the largest Bantam breeds. Buff Orpingtons come in buff, white, blue, and black colors.

Pros

- Very calm roosters with a steady temperament. They are not noisy or bossy.

- Love attention and will seek you out for cuddles. They are very patient with children and tolerate handling very well.

- Tolerate confinement very well, so they are perfect for small backyards in cities.

- Stay calm in new environments and do not mind unusual sounds or frequent handling. This makes them magnificent show birds.

- Can survive very cold temperatures.

- Love eating with humans and expect to share your food.

- Very protective of their chicks. They sometimes give mother hens a rest by brooding their eggs.

- Mature enough to be meat birds by week twenty-two.

- Fluffy and quite big, making them difficult for predators to kill. They will also give up their lives to fight a predator to protect the hens. They are highly watchful for predators and will alert the other flock if they see one.

- Very attentive towards the hens in a flock.

Cons

- Do not like high temperatures. They are large birds, so you must provide them plenty of space, ventilation, and shade.

- Can quickly die if their feathers get wet in winter.

- Have a powerful beak that can do damage, even to a human, if they are provoked.

- Will overeat and become obese without your constant supervision.

- Can be lazy, so keep them in the yard as much as possible to promote exercise. They forage for food when they need to.

- Need to check regularly for mites and lice in their extra-dense fur. You may need to treat them regularly with poultry dust, as it is hard to find such parasites on their feathers otherwise.

Faverolle Roosters

You will need to check regularly for mites and lice in their extra-dense fur. You may need to treat them regularly with poultry dust, as it is hard to find such parasites on their feathers otherwise.

Faverolles are French-origin chickens known for their fluffy, feathery beards. They have very loose and fluffy feathers that make them appear more prominent. They also have feathered legs like Brahma roosters.

Faverolle roosters look significantly different from Faverolle hens. The hens are usually two-toned, sporting white, gold, ginger feathers, and a beard. The roosters are more regal-looking. On average, weighing eight pounds on average, the Faverolle rooster sports a black beard, black undercarriage, and a black breast. On the other hand, he also wears straw-colored hackles (the neck and shoulder region), back, and saddle feathers. The wing has a deep gold color on the bow (top), with a triangular white tip.

Its tail is usually beetle green, its leg feathers are black, and its "under fluff" is slate gray. Faverolle roosters have many colors to their feathers that make them look like royalty.

Pros

- Have a very regal personality and are very calm, gentle, happy-go-lucky, and non-aggressive.

- A very healthy bird breed.

- Like both confinement and free-ranging.

- Make great pets and are very funny to watch. They love being petted and fussed over.

- Take outstanding care of hens in their flock and guard very well against predators. They look out for danger while foraging and alert the flock if they see anything dangerous.

Cons

- Mature a bit faster than other breeds.

- Usually friendly and happy, they can sometimes have grumpy personalities.

- Feathered legs and beards make them prone to lice. You will need to check them regularly to spot lice infestations early.

- When you treat them with poultry dust, you must be extra careful not to dust around their eyes and beaks, as this irritates them.

- Feathered legs are prone to scaly leg mites. As a feathered-foot breed, you will need to inspect their legs regularly for scaly leg mites. Be very thorough, as it is challenging to spot scaly leg mites in feather-foot breeds. If you do not spot them on time, the infection gets harder to control.

- Only live for five to seven years, which can be difficult if you become attached to them.

Plymouth Rock Roosters

Plymouth Rock roosters have equal black and white barring and feathers that end dark tips. Plymouth Rock hens have slightly wider black bars than the white bars, sometimes giving them a somewhat darker grey hue than roosters. The Barred Plymouth Rock is the most popular Plymouth Rock chicken variety. They can weigh up to nine and a half pounds, while bantam varieties can weigh up to three pounds.

Pros

- Are considered the "workhorses" of chickens. They do excellent jobs as roosters, protecting your hens from predators.

- Very calm and dependable roosters and cut an impressive figure as roosters in your yard because of their large size.

Cons

- You will need to give their large combs and wattles special care in the colder months to avoid frostbite.

Welsummer Roosters

Welsummers are popular in the United Kingdom and Australia. They are a relatively new breed, dating just under a hundred years ago. Today, they are only just gaining popularity in the United States.

They have a distinctive appearance, with long black sickle feathers and tail feathers, a beetle green chest and under feathers, and beautiful chestnut feathers everywhere else. Welsummer roosters weigh about seven pounds.

Pros

- Very intelligent, calm and friendly. They do not display territorial problems.

- In the middle of the pecking order, yet do not act overly bossy with other chickens.

- Prefer to forage in the yard than to be confined in a coop.

- Have no known significant health issues. They are very healthy and can live up to nine years.

- Very self-sufficient birds.

- Sometimes use their feathers as camouflage against predators.

Cons

- Very noisy; sometimes, they are upset, sometimes because they just feel like being loud. Your neighbors may not like living next to a noisy Welsummer rooster.

- Fare better in cooler, fall months and need access to shade to withstand the heat.

- Their combs and waffles are prone to frostbite in winter.

Apart from chicken breeds and varieties, there is another way to gauge the temperament and personality of chickens: the breeder. Some breeders like to breed gentle birds, while others prefer to breed more dominating chickens. I suggest speaking with the breeder about the personalities and temperaments of their chickens are. Ask about the father of the chicks you would like to buy, as this is the best predictor of the disposition of the rooster you are purchasing.

For example, Welsummer roosters are known for being calm and gentle. Yet, this is what one backyard chicken enthusiast, Val (The Happy Chicken Coop, 2021), had to say:

> "[We were mistakenly sent a Welsummer by accident with our batch of hens. Sad to say, he became very mean. At about 5-months-old, he began to beat up the hens. He ripped the comb almost completely off from one of the hens. We could not keep him.]."

Sourcing Chicks

You will need a good source for your chicks once you decide to start your flock. A good supplier will also save you a lot of time when you need to add a new chick to your existing flock. There are a few sources to consider when looking to acquire a chick:

A Local Breeder

Your local breeder is the best source for chicks. You will be supporting your local farmer, protecting local chicken heritage, and keeping rare chickens from becoming endangered.

You will be able to find a local breeder through word of mouth, especially among backyard chicken enthusiasts and local merchants. Consider asking your local vet or your local pet equipment store. If there are backyard chicken enthusiasts in your local area, you may be able to source rare or fun chick breeds from them.

You may also be able to find a local breeder in local advertisements in the newspaper, community leaflets, or Craigslist adverts. You can also contact the American Poultry Association to ask about the next poultry show in your local area. You will be able to find local breeders there. The Livestock Conservancy has an online directory of people that offer rare animal breeds in the country.

A Local Feed Store

Your local feed store may have some sexed chicks. Unfortunately, these chicks are often shipped, which stresses them out. However, you will be supporting local businesses.

Local feed stores allow you to buy as many birds as possible without worrying about shipping limitations or minimum purchase quantity. If you take your sexed chick home and find out it's a rooster, you can also return it, compared to buying from a local breeder. However, not all local stores accept returns, so you may have to rehome a rooster if you mistakenly buy one.

Online

If you have no other options, you will have to buy your chicks online, even though shipping them causes stress.

Day-old chicks can live on the nutrition from the yolk for about twenty-four hours. This is why they can be shipped to you speedily during the narrow twenty-four-hour window right after they hatch. Use shipping that guarantees door delivery before twenty-four hours, and be prepared to reach the post office as soon as the chicks arrive.

Purchasing chicks online is not feasible if you only want one or two chicks. As discussed in Chapter One, chicks need plenty of warmth to survive. Most companies have a minimum amount of chicks that you must purchase to ensure that the chicks stay warm during transit. You can buy a smaller quantity of chicks from My Pet Chicken or Meyer Hatchery.

What Is a Broody Hen?

A broody hen is a hen whose motherly instinct has kicked in. She is desperate for her eggs to hatch and will sit on her eggs (and sometimes stolen eggs) all day. Instinct, hormones, and maturity are causes of broodiness.

Broodiness shares similarities with nesting, commonly seen in pregnant women in their last trimester, who instinctively begin readying their house for their soon-to-arrive baby. Of course, if there is no rooster in your flock, the eggs will never hatch, but the instincts to brood are strong regardless.

A broody hen will stay in her nest all day and never go back to roost with the rest of the chickens in the evening. She may also pick out her breast feathers to transfer her body heat to the eggs. She will likely become very territorial. She will puff out her feathers in warning and squawk at anything that tries to come near her or her eggs. If you try to move her, she will peck you and try to bite you, so make sure you wear gloves.

A broody hen can be a problem if you do not want chicks. To add to this issue, once a hen becomes broody, she stops laying eggs as well. Potentially the most threatening consequence is that your other hens will go broody once one hen goes broody, leaving you with no fresh daily eggs.

Breaking a broody hen is a lot of hard work, so I try not to have my hens go broody in the first place. To do this, I always remove all eggs from their nesting boxes as soon as they are laid. I also do not allow my hens into the nesting box after laying their eggs for that day. This is sometimes impossible, so there will be moments when you need to "break" your hen in an emotionally healthy way.

Some backyard chicken enthusiasts recommend you leave a broody hen for twenty-one days. Eggs hatch after twenty-one days, causing your hen to stop being broody after that. However, in my experiences, my hens have not stopped being broody after this amount of time.

To break a broody hen, I remove her from the nest and place her with the rest of the flock. I like to move broody hens during feeding time when they're more likely to be distracted. I always wear gloves because a broody hen will fight back to defend her eggs. Every time the hen tries to go back to the nest, I pick her up and move her back to the rest of the hens.

If my hen is still broody after a few days of moving her from the nesting box, I block the entrance of the nesting box so she cannot fit inside, or I nail a piece of wood to the entrance. I also remove the nesting straw out of the box. This usually works to snap my broody hen out of her maternal instinct. If it does not work, I move her from the nesting box area to the roosting area during sunset. Chickens are generally too scared to move around during the dark. If my hen is adamant about sitting in the nesting box, I place a bag of frozen vegetables under her. Hens get broody because their body temperature rises. By cooling her body heat with the frozen vegetables, her brain might interpret this as a sign she is no longer broody.

My final option is to use a broody cage if no other option works. This is a cage with a wire bottom. I prefer to use a dog or cat carrier with the bottom cut out and replaced with chicken wire. I place my broody hen in the cage with only food and water. There is also no bedding in the cage and plenty of natural daylight around. Finally, I position the cage on a raised base using wood or cement blocks. If my hen lays an egg before three days pass, I know she is no longer broody.

If I let her out after three days and she returns to the nesting box, I keep her in the broody cage for another three days to make sure she is broken.

FOUR

PROVIDING THE PROPER NOURISHMENT

"My first business deal was with my mother. I invested in chickens. I sold the eggs to my mother."

-Joel McCrea

LIKE EVERY OTHER LIVING THING, CHICKENS NEED PROPER food, water, and nutrients to stay healthy. Your chicks will need specific diet requirements at different stages of a chick's development. Starter rations (for chicks from hatching to eight weeks old) are high in protein with a twenty-four percent protein content, making them quite expensive. After this stage, grower (eight to fourteen weeks) and finisher (fifteen to eighteen weeks) rations are lower in protein, with a twenty percent and eighteen percent protein content. This is because older birds require less protein.

Once your chicken reaches adulthood (eighteen or more weeks), she will continue to need proper nutrition to lay good quality eggs and to live a good life. There are many do's and don'ts for feeding chickens; for example, you will have to feed your chicks differently depending on if you want to grow them for meat, egg-laying, or breeding. The wrong diet can cause long-term health problems for your birds.

Although domestication has led to healthier flocks, modern chickens need a more extensive diet because they have been selectively bred to produce more eggs and more meat. Most backyard chicken enthusiasts would advise you to avoid commercial bird feed. It is often unhealthy and makes health claims that it cannot achieve. It usually contains antibiotics and arsenicals that promote health and improve growth, coccidiostats for combating coccidiosis, and occasionally mold inhibitors as well. When feeding these to your chickens, it becomes difficult for you to control the number of synthetic chemicals that your birds are ingesting.

If you decide to use commercial bird feed, it should be pelleted so your birds can eat more at one time. Chickens are nibblers. They prefer to make frequent trips to the feed trough for small meals. These frequent trips require energy. When feed is pelleted, it reduces the amount of energy your chicken uses to feed because it reduces the number of trips your bird takes. However, others in the industry believe that a pasture-based, natural approach to backyard chicken farming is better. This includes meals where the chicken receives more exercise.

Whether confined, free-range, or a combination of the two, your chickens need to be fed with a balanced pelleted ration. Their diet should contain a significant proportion of corn for energy, soybean meal for protein, and vitamin and mineral supplements. There is a lot of inaccurate information about feeding your birds, so you must ensure that you're always following the most up-to-date scientific recommendations concerning chicken feed.

Finally, your chickens should receive clean water at all times. Giving your poultry water with levels of total dissolved solids above 3000 ppm can be harmful to their health and reduce egg production.

Starter Diets

Newborn chicks need a feed that contains eighteen–twenty percent protein for their growth and health. If you are using commercial feed, you can choose between medicated and non-medicated feed, depending on your need to protect your chicken from diseases. If you decide to make your feed or use unmedicated feed, you can add natural supplements to their feed to medicate your chicks naturally. A sprinkle of probiotic powder will help combat coccidia, and a sprinkle of garlic powder will add antibacterial and antiviral properties. Sea kelp, a sprinkle of brewer's yeast, and an assortment of fresh chopped or dried culinary herbs like oregano, rosemary, sage, and parsley will strengthen your chicks' immune system.

Chicks have small beaks, so do not use pellets. Instead, use crumbles, which are larger pellets broken down into smaller sizes. Introduce small chick-sized grits into their diet, or use coarse mixed sand or dirt. As discussed in Chapter One, chickens need grit to digest their food. Additionally, avoid calcium-based foods in a chicken's diet. A high-calcium diet may cause kidney stones, reducing the lifespan of your chickens.

I am cautious when giving water to my chicks at this stage. I include stones or marbles in their waterer so they will not drown if they fall in. Other tips about water and hydration are discussed later in this chapter.

I also like to treat my chicks once in a while. They enjoy treats like moistened oats, chopped weeds, soft scrambled eggs, and minced garlic.

Grower Diets

Between eight to fourteen weeks, a grower chicken needs two percent less protein. Their diet should be made up of sixteen–eighteen percent protein. You will then have to switch to a feed called layer feed or grower rotation. Your chickens will be big enough to eat pellets at this stage. They will also need commercial grit added to their diet or coarse dirt and small stones. If you use homemade or unmedicated pellets, you will need to add the same supplements as the starter diet (including food-grade diatomaceous earth or silica). It is packed full of minerals and prevents external parasites, such as mites, lice, and fleas, from infesting your chickens' feathers.

They still need to drink diluted apple cider vinegar (ACV) water twice a week. I like to add fruit and vegetables to their diet, including cucumbers, leafy greens, corn, peas, and watermelons. I also give them cooked brown rice and whole-grain pasta. However, be careful and thoughtful when adding new foods to their diet; read further in this chapter to see a list of foods that can be dangerous to your chickens.

Finisher Diets

Between the ages of fifteen to eighteen weeks, chickens need about sixteen percent protein. If you are unable to find finisher feed, you can use grower feed at this stage. My hens are usually free-ranging by now, so they are able to get stones for their diet by foraging. They still need cool, diluted ACV water twice a week. If you are using natural homemade feed or unmedicated pellets, continue using the same supplements as you would with a grower diet, but increase them by two percent.

It would be best if you continued to give your chickens healthy treats in moderation, adding things like cracked corn, sunflower seeds, and mealworms.

Layer Diets

Hens typically begin laying eggs between weeks sixteen and eighteen. During this time, they must consume finisher feed that meets their nutritional requirements. A few weeks after a chicken begins laying eggs, I begin to give them layer feed. This will typically take place sometime during the twenty-second week.

Layer feed is specially formulated to help layer hens produce the best quality eggs. It contains 1 percent crude protein and a high calcium diet to help the eggshells form. If you feed a layer hen a layer diet before they begin producing eggs, this will reduce their egg production in the long term. Furthermore, if you provide a layer hen grower feed, they will produce fewer eggs at a lower quality.

Making Natural Feed

You can mix your own feed rations at home. This ensures that only natural ingredients are used. However, preparing a balanced diet for your chickens can be complicated and expensive, especially if you have a limited background in nutrition. You will need specialized knowledge if you are creating your own feed. As a beginner backyard chicken enthusiast, this is information that you do not have yet.

Furthermore, making feed takes a lot of time. You will need to source feed ingredients, then mill and mix them according to your well-balanced and nutritious formula, then have the formula pelleted. I will recommend you stick to store-bought feed. Once you are more experienced with raising chickens, you can learn how to make feed. Chickens who don't eat well-balanced feed suffer nutritional imbalances and health problems.

. . .

Feeding Senior Chickens

If you have senior chickens in your flock, you can buy feed specially formulated for aging chickens. These are relatively new formulas and are not yet as popular as other chicken feed formulas. Nonetheless, many backyard chicken enthusiasts bond with their pets and often live with them even after they mature and no longer produce eggs or tender meat. So, you may need to know how to feed senior chickens.

A mature hen will not need as much protein or calcium in her diet as a layer hen in her prime. I offer my older hens crushed eggshells, sage, black oil sunflower seeds, and wheat to add some calcium to their diet. Rice, millet, wheat, meat scraps, and scrambled eggs are also good protein sources for mature hens. This will enable muscle development while keeping their bones, cartilage, blood, feathers, and skin healthy and well-maintained. Finally, your older hens will need more carbs during colder months to stay warm. Older birds are easily stressed. The vitamins in their carb-laden scratch grains strengthen their immune systems and help them deal with stress.

Frequently Asked Questions

Q: How much protein do meat chickens need?

A: Meat chickens need a specific type of feed known as broiler feed. You can purchase starter, grower, or finisher broiler feed.

Broiler feed is dense in protein, causing your chickens to grow very big in a short time. The protein in broiler feed is too much for layer hens and will cause serious health problems. Broilers need plenty of food, so give them twenty-four-seven access to food to encourage weight gain.

Q: How can I make an edible pecking block treat for my chickens?

A: Pecking block recipes are effortless to make. You can serve them warm, at room temperature, or frozen during the hotter months to cool your chickens down. This is how I make an edible block treat for my flock:

Ingredients:

2 cups meat scraps

1 cup fat, preferably lard or coconut oil

1 cup chicken feed

1 cup chicken scratch

1 cup oats

1 cup cornmeal

1/2 cup seeds, black oil sunflower seeds

) mealworms

1 cup molasses

1/2 cup eggshells, ground

1/4 cup applesauce

Four eggs

Directions

- Preheat the oven to 400°F.
- Mix all the ingredients in a large bowl. Combine well.
- Pour the mixture into an 8 inch × 8 inch or a 9 inch × 9 inch pan.
- Create a small hole, big enough for a string to go through. You will use this hole to hang up the block later.
- Bake for 30 minutes, or until the block is stiff and crusty on top.
- Allow to cool and give to the chickens when ready. If you do not plan to give it to the chickens right away, you can freeze or refrigerate it for later use.

Q: What is unmedicated feed?

A: You can buy medicated or unmedicated starter and grower chicken feed. Medicated chicken feed is made with amprolium, which prevents coccidiosis and other diseases in chicks. If you have vaccinated your chicks for coccidiosis, you must use unmedicated feed. Amprolium is very incompatible with the ingredients in the vaccination. You may also choose to forgo medicated feed because you cannot manage the amount of medication given to your chickens. In this case, you can use unmedicated feed and add supplements that do the job of the medicine.

Q: What is chicken mash?

A: Mash is a loose, unprocessed type of chicken feed. I feed it to my baby chicks because it is effortless to digest. Sometimes I serve it to adult chickens, too. Once in a while, I add hot water to make a porridge-like dish using chicken mash. Chickens love mash porridge.

Q: What is chicken scratch?

A: Chicken scratch combines corn with other grains to create a different type of chicken feed. It contains plenty of energy and helps your chickens stay warm on colder nights. It is not to be fed to chickens regularly, rather as a treat or a supplement for days when your flock needs a little more energy from their diet. If you use it as a regular diet, your chickens will quickly become overweight, especially if they are not free-range chickens.

Q: How can I cut the cost of chicken feed?

A: You can cut the cost of chicken feed by fermenting it first. Fermenting chicken feed can be done naturally by simply soaking chicken feed for a few days in a glass or BPA-free container filled with dechlorinated or filtered water.

Fermentation releases many of the grains' nutrients, leading to healthy chickens and better quality eggs. It is also denser, allowing your birds to feel full for longer and cutting the quantity of feed you need. You may feed your chickens fermented food for every meal if you wish, although fermented scratch should still only be a treat or supplementary meal.

Q: What fruit and vegetables can I feed my chickens?

A: Free-range hens eat a lot of greens already found in the backyard. They may not need any additional nutrients from fruit and vegetables, although you may still feed them to your chickens as occasional treats. However, confined layer hens will need the nutrients from fruit and vegetables. You can feed them cabbage, cucumbers, chard, chickweed, broccoli, kale, bok choy, endive, melon, squash, strawberries, vegetable peels, and fruit peels.

Q: What foods should I avoid?

A: Fatty foods. As discussed by Freedom Ranger Hatchery, Inc. (2021), if your hens consume too many fatty foods, it can lead to Fatty Liver Hemorrhagic Syndrome. Fatty Liver Hemorrhagic Syndrome may lead to sudden death for your hens. It typically occurs when your chicken becomes overweight, causing fat to build around their liver. This then makes the liver soft and prone to bleeding.

Apricots. The leaves and pit of apricots are also toxic to chickens. They contain cyanogenic glycosides, which can trigger breathing problems, low blood pressure, and seizures. If you have an apricot tree in your yard, fence it with a tall fence so that your chickens cannot reach it.

Avocados. Avocados can cause sudden death in chickens. They contain a toxin called persin. Persin has been linked to myocardial necrosis in chickens, a condition that results when the heart stops beating.

Onions. Onions in large quantities cause the build-up of thiosulfate, a type of salt that can destroy red blood cells, causing anemia or jaundice. This jaundice is sometimes fatal.

Uncooked beans. Cooked beans are safe for chickens. However, raw beans contain hemagglutinin, which is toxic to chickens.

Apple seeds. Apple seeds are well known for containing cyanide. Since chickens are relatively smaller animals, just a few apple seeds can contain enough cyanide to kill a chicken.

Excess salt. Salt is not a natural part of a chicken's diet, so they can quickly get salt poison. Reduce excess salt by only feeding them scraps with a low salt concentration.

Moldy food. Moldy food will make your chickens sick or cause them to die—this includes stale bread and overripe fruits.

Chocolate. Chocolate contains methylxanthine theobromine, an alkaloid that is toxic to chickens.

Citrus fruits. You can feed citrus fruits to your chickens in moderation. If you give them too many, it will reduce the number of eggs your chickens produce.

Nightshade plants. Avoid feeding your chickens any raw plant that belongs in the nightshade family. They contain solanine or sometimes oxalic acid, two highly toxic compounds to chickens, sometimes causing kidney failure. When you cook these plants, it breaks down these poisonous acids. Potatoes, rhubarb leaves, tomatoes, and eggplants all belong in the nightshade family of plants.

Toxic garden plants. If you plan to keep chickens in your backyard, you will need to check that your chickens do not have access to plants that are toxic to them. Generally, your chickens will naturally stay away from plants that are toxic to them. Keeping poisonous garden plants away from reach is a failsafe plan nonetheless. These plants include: Amaranthus Palmeri, azaleas, belladonna (also known as deadly nightshade), bloodroot, bull nettle, bracken fern, bryony, bulbs (including tulips, irises, daffodils, and narcissuses), castor bean, cocklebur, curly dock, delphinium, fern, foxglove, hemlock tree, holly, horse chestnut, horseradish, hyacinth, hydrangea, ivy, laburnum seed, lantana, lily of the valley, lobelia, lupine, oak trees and acorns, periwinkle, rhododendron, John's wort, water hemlock, and yew.

Hydrating Your Chickens

Chickens need clean water to produce energy for growing, molting, laying eggs, growing feathers, and every other biological process. Without regular water access, a chicken will not get enough water into the crop it eats, causing it to dry in the chicken's stomach and halt digestion. Chickens' droppings are very moist and wet. Without regular and plentiful water, this will cause problems with waste removal.

Your chickens will fall ill if their water is not clean. Chickens are very prone to water-borne illnesses and diseases, some of which are fatal. Clean water improves their immune system, keeping germs and bacteria away. You may also use rainwater, but you have to store it in black-lidded barrels until it is time for use.

In cool weather, your chickens can survive up to forty-eight hours without water. They are very low maintenance. However, in hotter weather, you will need to make sure that they are well-watered at all times. If you live in a hot climate, your chickens may only be able to survive for eight hours without water since your chickens rely on water to regulate their temperature.

No matter where you live or what season it is, it is in your best interest to water your chickens regularly. If not, laying hens may stop laying eggs or produce low-quality eggs resulting from heat stress. Chicken eggs are made up of seventy percent water and cannot form properly without sufficient water.

Do not go more than six hours without watering your chickens (or chicks) to be on the safe side. If you do not provide your chickens with enough water regularly, you will get in trouble with the law. As another protective measure, provide 1000 ml of water per chicken every day. Indoor chickens do not need more than 250 ml of water daily, so this measure assures you that your chickens are well-watered. To ensure that my chickens have enough water, I typically fill up the waterers in my coop and in my backyard every morning to ensure each chicken gets 1000 ml. That way, if I am busy or forget to re-water for that day, I know that my chickens will all have more than enough water to sustain them for the day.

Do not leave water in the coop overnight, as it can lead to dampness in the house. The water will evaporate into the coop walls and the bedding. Leaving water overnight will also attract mice that will infect your chickens with bacteria and even feed on your chicks. It is also very likely that a chicken may cause some to pour or splatter everywhere. Leaving chickens without water overnight is not a problem because chickens can go overnight without drinking water. However, you will have to give them water first thing in the morning.

Colder Months

During the winter months, your flock's water runs the risk of freezing. While chickens may swallow snow to hydrate themselves, they cannot drink enough water from snow. Furthermore, snow can be dangerous to chickens if it contains bacteria or other hazardous microorganisms. To prevent this problem, I replace the water every time it freezes. I also use an electrically heated chicken waterer when the temperature is extremely cold. Keep in mind that it might be challenging to replace the water if it becomes frozen in the water container; an electric water heater is your best choice in this case.

Electric water heaters are thermostatically controlled, stopping ice from forming. When I use them, I check them periodically because my chickens sometimes unplug them out of curiosity. Additionally, the heat from your electric water heater sometimes does not distribute evenly in my waterer, causing icy layers to form, preventing water from flowing. Therefore, I regularly check my water bowl to ensure that the chickens are still receiving water.

If you live in a region with freezing winters, you can rotate your waterers every twelve hours. You can leave one waterer inside to stay warm while the other stays in the coop, rotating both waterers every twelve hours so the frozen one can thaw.

Warmer Months

You do not want your chickens drinking from water heated up by the sun. This will neither refresh nor cool them down. To keep my hens refreshed in the heat, I change their water regularly and add ice cubes several times a day. I make sure that they are drinking cool water in hot temperatures. If it gets extremely hot, you should speak with your vet about adding electrolytes to their water.

Apart from ice cubes, there are other ways to hydrate and refresh your chickens when it's hot. I give my chickens frozen treats that will keep them cool and hydrated. To make a delicious and refreshing frozen treat, I add berries to water and freeze them. This creates a hydrating summer snack that also doubles as a toy for my chickens. They love to peck at the frozen berries in the ice. Sometimes I also give them frozen slices of watermelon and other frozen fruits that double up as treats. If neither of these options are available, I chop up some fresh grass and greens, like cabbage or their favorite plants around the garden and backyard. I add them into a bowl of cold water then serve it to them. My hens have fun picking out the greens at the same time as they are hydrating themselves.

Water and Hydration Tips

- Use two or more water sources so that all your chickens will have enough to drink. Chickens at the top of the pecking order will bully the more docile ones out of the water if there is just one waterer. It will also keep you from refilling waterers all day, especially in hot weather.

- Always make sure your waterers are clean to avoid passing harmful microorganisms to your chickens. Use elevated waterers that are just low enough for the chickens to reach. That way, they can comfortably drink water without getting any dirt into the water when they scratch themselves.

- Keep water containers in the shade. The water will heat up if left in the sun, making it undrinkable. It will also evaporate faster in the sun, forcing you to refill the water containers more than usual.

- Hide waterers away from the line of sight of wild birds and other wild animals that also get thirsty. They will drink the water, leaving none for your chickens.

- Use chicken watering systems that hold a lot of water, like a vacuum-sealed galvanized drinker, and place a few of them around your yard and inside your coop. This will stop you from worrying about your chickens running out of water every few hours because your flock will have a few days' supply of water at their disposal.

- Watering systems are also beneficial because chickens do not drink large amounts all at once. They can take in small amounts frequently during the day whenever they need.

- Add a splash of apple cider vinegar (ACV) to their water a few times per week to supply your chicks with gut-friendly probiotics (good bacteria), healthy vitamins and minerals, and even trace elements. Do not use ACV in metal waterers. It may react to some metals (for example, galvanized metals), causing them to leech zinc into the water. Zinc is toxic to birds.

- Diluted apple cider vinegar water also refreshes your chickens on very hot days and supports their health when they are stressed. Undiluted apple cider vinegar water also helps to reduce fecal and intestinal odor by breaking down minerals and fats that assimilate protein into the body. It also increases the acidity of the chickens' digestive tract (this reduces your flocks' chances of catching common infections and increases their resistance to diseases). It prevents the build-up of green algae in plastic waterers in hotter months.

FIVE

TIME TO BRING HOME THE BABIES

"The domesticated chicken is probably the most widespread bird in the annals of planet Earth. If you measure success in terms of numbers, chickens, cows and pigs are the most successful animals ever."

-Yuval Noah Harari

BRINGING HOME A BABY CHICK REQUIRES CARE AND planning if you want your chicks to survive and thrive. Like all baby animals, chicks are delicate and need extra care from their caretaker. You are your chicks' caretaker, so your new chicks are relying on you for their survival. This chapter focuses on what you'll need to create a temporary indoor coop for your new chicks, as well as the health, safety, daily care, and food required to care for baby chicks.

Building a Brooder

You need a brooder for when your baby chicks arrive. A brooder keeps your chicks contained, warm, and dry. It is a simple setup that includes a bottom surface covered with bedding, a heat lamp, a top to stop them from flying out, and the chicks' food and water.

When you keep your chicks in a brooder, you keep them quarantined. By quarantining your chicks, you are sure that they are not carrying any diseases or infections when you introduce them to the rest of your flock.

During their time in the brooder, I watch out for:

- Signs of lice or mites

- Dull or shriveled combs

- Blocked nostrils

- Fluid coming from their eyes

- Scaly legs

During their time in the brooder, I watch out for:

- Signs of lice or mites

- Dull or shriveled combs

- Blocked nostrils

- Fluid coming from their eyes

- Scaly legs

If I notice any of these things, I take the sick chick(s) to the vet as soon as possible. I always wash my hands thoroughly after handling my chicks and my chickens. This prevents diseases and infections from spreading from both sides.

To create a good brooder, you will need:

A Container

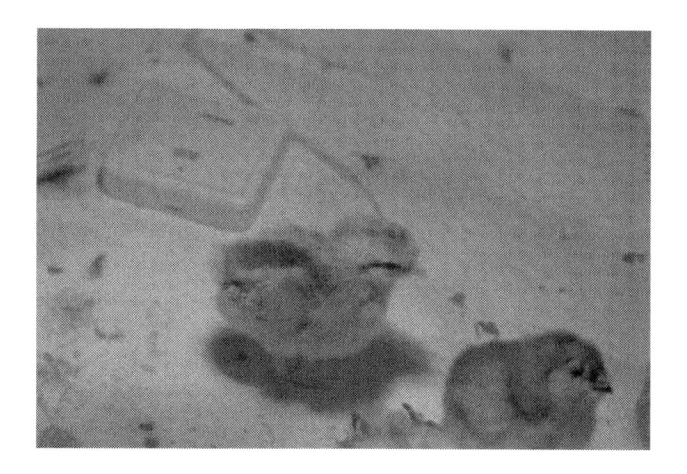

It is relatively easy to improvise when building a brooder. You can use a simple cardboard box, a regular wooden box, a small bucket, a kiddie pool, a feeding trough, a plastic storage tub, a fish tank, or anything else that meets the requirements for a brooder's setup. You will need to factor in space when setting up your brooder: you will need about two square feet of space per chick. Cramping your chicks into the brooder will stress them out, which may cause other issues for the chicks as they grow up. You will need to upsize as your chicks get larger. If you use a cardboard box, make sure you place them in a safe place, without any other added risk of fire hazards, such as books or leaflets. (I will discuss fire hazards later in this chapter.)

If you have pets or children around, use a lid on the brooder. Using a bucket or any other container that is at least twelve inches deep is advantageous because it stops your chicks from being able to fly out without using a lid. You have to use a breathable cover, like a net, to ensure that your chicks do not suffocate.

A Heat Lamp

A brooder lamp will keep the chicks at the right temperature. Use a 250-watt infrared heat lamp with a red bulb as your heat lamp of choice. An infrared brooder lamp is more efficient than a white one because it does not prevent your chicks from sleeping. It calms your chicks, helping prevent them from picking on each other. You can find brooder heat lamps at feed stores and hardware stores.

It would be best to purchase a reflector and a clamp to mount the bulb. I also buy an accompanying wire guard to prevent fire hazards, which goes underneath the bulb. The guard ensures a decreased chance of a fire if the lamp falls on the shavings. I make it extra secure by attaching it safely at my desired height using a chain. I loop the wire over a beam or hook, then secure it using a wide plastic tie. Finally, I duct tape it too! If you have the clamp-on type of heat lamp, use the same methods for securing it. It takes less than two minutes to start a fire with a heat lamp. They are the number one cause of coop fires and deaths every year, so I take fire security seriously.

The closer you place the lamp to the brooder, the warmer it gets for the chicks. Before my chicks arrive, I use a thermometer as a gauge to place the lamp at the best height for my chicks. The optimal temperatures for each week are:

- Week One: 90–95° F
- Week Two: 85–90° F
- Week Three: 80–85° F
- Week Four: 75–80° F
- Week Five: 70–75° F
- Week Six: 70° F
- Week Seven: 65° F

I also create a system to easily adjust the height of the lamp every week. Using a piece of chain and an S hook works well. The warmth of a brooder will be affected by the number of hatchlings within it as well as the temperature of the room. If I have many hatchlings or relatively warm in the room, I move the lamp further from the chicks. The more chicks you have, the more they will stay together to keep each other warm.

Furthermore, if I am brooding in the middle of a very hot summer, I may not need a brooder lamp at all, depending on the temperature in the room. As mentioned above, keep your brooder draft-free. Draft in any part of the brooder can cause health problems for your chicks. I always use a thermometer to make sure that all areas of my brooder are at the right temperature at all times.

The best indicators of whether the brooder is too warm or too cold are the hatchlings themselves.

- They are too hot if they are away from the brooder lamp, spread out around the walls of the brooder, and panting. Chicks who are too hot can develop problems including dehydration and pasty butt, a condition where droppings stick to the chick's vent area, preventing the excretion of waste. If this is the case, lower the temperature in the room or move the lamp higher.

- If they are huddled close together, near the brooder lamp, they are too cold. In this case, they will peep loudly. Chicks do not yet have feathers that can protect them from the cold. They can die quickly if cold, so you must keep a close eye out for signs that they are too cold. Increase the heat in your brooder or increase the temperature in the room until the chicks are warm.

- Chicks that are comfortable will look happy and act carefree. They will eat, drink, explore and walk around the brooder cheerfully, without signs of distress.

Typically the chicks will no longer need a heat lamp at some point between weeks seven and twelve. However, there are other signals that your chicks can now survive independently. They are:

- The breed of chicken. Heavier breeds require less heat than smaller breeds, especially bantam chicks.

- Your chicks have gone through the second molt, grown enough feathers, and are no longer forced to keep warm with just their original down feathers.

- Where you live and the time of year. If it is summer and you're living in Arizona, you likely won't need a heat lamp at all. You may need a heat lamp for just a couple of weeks in warm areas.

- Your chicks are now spending time away from the heat lamp, choosing to spend days staying as far away from the heat lamp as they can.

Thermometer

I use a thermometer with a wire and sensor to easily read the temperature from the edge of the brooder, while the sensor sits right under the lamp. The chicks are very curious at this age and will peck at the wire. This should not cause any damage, however. You can also tuck the wire under some shavings to hide it from the chicks.

Bedding

Pine shavings are great beddings for your brooder. If you use a container with a slippery base, such as a plastic box, layer paper towels underneath the pine shavings. The chicks will then be able to keep their balance for the first few days.

Spread one-two inches of pine shavings to keep the chicks happy. You will need to change the bedding daily to keep it clean and free of animal droppings. Remember that chicks' immune systems are not yet fully developed, so you want to keep them as free of germs and microorganisms as possible. You must dispose of wet litter immediately as they cause mold that can lead to pneumonia. Place the chicks in a non-slippery container that they ca not fly over while you change their bedding.

Do not use cedar shavings because the are toxic to poultry. Do not use newspapers because newspapers are slippery, and the chicks can develop spraddle legs as a result. The chicks can also swallow newspaper shavings, putting their health in jeopardy. Other bedding you can use includes finely shredded paper, peat moss, crushed corn cobs, or chopped straw.

Feeders And Waterers

Whether through feeders or small plastic tubs which you have in your house, there needs to be enough feeder space for all chicks to eat at one time. Large pans or containers are not suitable since the chicks will walk through the feed, leaving droppings on the food. Buy feeders made for chicks because they are designed to prevent the chicks from leaving droppings in their food. You can avoid feed waste by filling the feeders only one-half full. If the chicks need more, you can add more feed.

As with adult chickens, you must keep the chicks' waterers filled every day. The height of the waterers needs to be raised as the chicks grow to prevent spillage into the brooder. Level the lip of the waterer, so it is even with the height of the chicks' back. This will keep the brooder from becoming damp or flooded. Chick waterers are shallow dishes to prevent them from drowning in the water. For additional safety, place a few pebbles or marbles in the water pan to stop your chicks from falling asleep face down in the water. You can remove the marbles after a couple of weeks.

The number of chicks you are getting should determine the feeders and waterers you use. A round, plastic, or metal feeder is perfect for a handful of chicks. For more, you'll need a trough chick feeder, which allows even chicks at the bottom of the pecking order to get enough to eat.

Return to Chapter Four to learn how to feed your chicks.

The Day Of Arrival

You have prepared your brooder for your chicks' arrival and are now waiting for them. There are a few steps to complete the day of their arrival to get them off to the best possible start in life. The most important thing is to be considerate of the chicks' needs. They are tired and stressed after just hatching and finding themselves in a new environment. Don't spook them by making loud noises. Your chicks are confused and weary at this point, so it's best to take them "home" immediately. They simply want three things: to eat, to drink, and to sleep.

I always turn on my heat lamp a few hours before the new chicks arrive. Then, I keep the temperature at the bottom of the brooder at 95 degrees Fahrenheit. The chicks are always happy with the warmth as soon as I place them in their new home. Before placing them in the brooder, I dip each chick's beak in the water in the feeder. This lets them know where to drink water and even how to drink water. Next, I place the water near the heat lamp, so it warms the water. Chicks love warm water and hate cold water. However, I do not put it directly under the heat lamp because this will cause the water to grow disease-carrying germs. To teach them where to get food, I scratch their feed with my fingers. The curious chicks will start to scratch and peck at it, leading to them eating the food.

I leave them for about thirty minutes then check on them again. If they have moved as far away from the heat lamp as possible, then I adjust it so that they are warm, but not too hot. If the temperature is just right, they will be scattered all over the brooder.

Signs Of Sickness

You can reduce the possibility of your chicks getting sick by keeping the brooder clean and dry. Other ways to reduce the likelihood of sickness are providing the proper diet, making sure your chicks are not too hot or too cold, and adding some natural supplements to your chicks' water (see Chapter Four). Despite your best efforts, your chicks might still fall sick, so you must be able to recognize signs of sickness when this happens. The quicker you respond to sickness symptoms, the greater the chance that your chicks will be fine. Signs of illness that you should keep an eye out for include:

- Your chick becomes uninterested in interacting with the other chicks.

- Your chick becomes inactive and sluggish.

- Your chick's droppings stick to their vent (butt). This is specifically a sign of Pasty Butt.

- Your chick spends too much time under the heat source, not even leaving to eat or drink.

- Your chick becomes unwilling to eat or drink.

Pasty butt is the most common sickness for baby chicks. Caused by stress, pasty butt can appear if your chick is too hot, too cold, being pecked at by other chicks, or any other causes of stress. Pasty can be fatal if it is not cleaned immediately because it prevents your chick from properly removing waste from its system. The blockage can be removed by carefully soaking or rinsing it in warm water and gently rubbing it off.

Introducing Your Chick to the Rest of the Flock

Once the chicks have grown their feathers, I introduce them to the rest of the flock. I typically wait until the chicks are of similar size (around weeks fifteen and sixteen) to the rest of the flock before introducing them. This way, I can skip the quarantine stage.

Do not introduce just one chick to the flock. This chick may be bullied if introduced alone. It is better to introduce a minimum of three baby chicks to the community. Chickens are social animals and thrive in groups of other birds of a similar age. Baby chicks help each other when they grow up together, so you will get healthier chicks when they are introduced in groups. Introducing more than three chicks will also make sure your chicks don't get lonely, in case one of them does not make it.

When introducing my chicks, I do not place them in the flock just like that. This will cause squabbling, and my chicks might be hurt by the chickens at the top of the pecking order. Instead, I introduce the chicks to the flock slowly. The first thing I do is I introduce the chicks to the free-range area, but I separate them from the other flock using a safe wire mesh or playpen. I make sure that the older chickens can spend a week or so getting used to the chicks' presence. Then, after a week, I remove the wire mesh and let the new chickens out to free-range. After a few minutes, I let the older chickens join the younger ones. You can use the same technique if you keep your chickens in a pen.

There will be some jostling when the two groups meet each other because they are fighting to establish a pecking order. This is normal, so I do not interfere unless one of my chickens starts bleeding or looks injured. I always watch closely so that I can separate the chickens if the jostling gets too violent or lasts more than a few minutes. Then I re-introduce them the next day. I do this once a day until they start to settle down within a few minutes of introducing them. Once my chickens have settled down, and the pecking order is established, I move the new chickens permanently into the coop with the older hens. Do not be surprised if some of your hens "go off lay" after introducing new chickens. (To go off lay means to suddenly stop laying eggs.) Chickens love routine and will go off lay for even the slightest changes in their daily routine. This should only last a few days.

I like to distract my older hens by making sure to fill their coop and the free-range area with treats and other distractions. A mirror or a chicken swing will divert your chicken's focus away from the new flock. My hens love hay and straw, so I give them a fresh supply to distract them from the younger chickens. I also provide my new chickens with "safe spaces" by raising my roosting bars and covered spaces so that my new chickens have areas where they can go to rest when they need privacy, feel too tired, or feel overwhelmed.

SIX

EGGS 101

"The happiest moments of my childhood were spent on my grandmother's front porch in Durham, N.C., or at her sister's farmhouse in Orange County, where chickens paraded outside the kitchen's screen door and hams were cured in the smokehouse."

-Andre Leon Talley

How do you collect and clean your eggs? How do you also store your eggs for optimum quality? And if you have an egg shortage, what can you do to remedy the situation?

Training Your Hens to Use Nesting Boxes

Like any other pet, it is best to train your hens at a young age. It takes time and effort to train any animal, so you will need to begin as soon as you notice that your hen is about to start laying eggs. Hens begin laying eggs when they are around four to five months old. They always show signs of change at this time, such as anxious, restless, and distracted behavior, where they meander from place to place, seemingly looking for a good place to build a nest.

Once you notice this, you will want to alert them to the nesting boxes' presence and purpose. I do so by placing golf balls in the nest boxes. These fool the hens into thinking these are eggs, helping them associate the nesting box with laying eggs. It may take a while to train my new hens, but once they are accustomed to this method, they are more than happy to use it continuously. I also sprinkle scratch or cracked corn in the box for a couple of days to lure the chicken into the nesting box. Once the chicken is inside the nesting box, she will experience how dark, quiet, and comfortable it is and choose to use it as her nest of her own free will. I keep the nesting boxes clean and always use fresh bedding to make them attractive to the hens. Your goal is to lure your chicken into using it, so do not leave dirt or waste matter in it. Your chicken will be unwilling to try a nesting box if her first use of the box is an unpleasant experience.

As with most animals, if you have older hens, the younger hens will copy the learned behaviors of the older ones: they will learn how to use the nesting boxes themselves.

Always treat your hens as individuals. Some hens are more feisty and independent and will refuse to lay in any nesting box, no matter what you do. This is not a cause for concern. In this case, I use a different training method that involves picking her up when I see her trying to lay an egg. Then I move her to a nest box to complete her egg-laying there. I do this a few times to help her associate laying eggs with the nesting box.

When And How Often to Collect Eggs

When collecting eggs, it is vital that they are safe, clean, and fresh. Make sure that the eggs you gather are as clean as possible. This will help you minimize the amount of egg-cleaning required later.

Always gather eggs as early and as often as possible. I try to collect eggs twice a day if I can manage it. Leaving eggs in the nesting boxes overnight will tempt your chickens to make a habit out of eating the eggs. One of the reasons why chickens begin eating raw eggs is egg breakage. If you leave eggs overnight, your chickens may accidentally step on them and get a taste for them. Egg breakage also happens because some chickens roost on the edges of the nest boxes, or even in them.

Even when I have no time, I always collect eggs early in the day. Most hens do not lay eggs past ten in the morning. This way, your flock has less time to accidentally step on their eggs or to eat them.

Do not go more than a day without collecting eggs. If you do, you will have to clean the broken eggs from the coop and risk having given your chickens a taste of raw eggs. Giving your chicken a taste of raw eggs is a lot of work that can be avoided by collecting eggs regularly. (Turn to Chapter Seven to learn why chickens eat eggs and how to prevent or stop them.)

Cleaning, Storing, and Refrigerating Eggs

Another potential issue to keep in mind when collecting eggs is the possibility of chickens pooping on the eggs. If too much poop gets on an egg, it can become inedible and even make you sick. If you find poop in the nest boxes when you are collecting eggs, clean it out very well and replace the straw or shavings. Learning how to clean your eggs properly will keep you and your family from getting sick.

There are two ways you can clean chicken eggs: dry cleaning and wet cleaning. Dry cleaning is better than wet cleaning because it does not wash off the egg's bloom (the antibacterial protective layer). When I dry clean, I wipe the eggs with an abrasive sponge or loofah. Some people even use fine sandpaper. No matter what you choose, these options remove all dirt and feces from the shell. Wet washing is still essential, and sometimes I use wet washing when the eggs are dirtier or have egg yolk stuck to the shells. Always wash your eggs under warm running water from a tap. Ensure the water is warmer than the egg's temperature, but make sure the water is not too hot. After wet washing, use a paper towel to dry the eggs, then place them in a clean, open carton, an egg basket, or a wire rack. Then you can sanitize the washed eggs by spraying them with a solution of bleach diluted with water.

If you are storing your eggs in the fridge, they can last for a month after the day of collection. Labeling your egg cartons will help you calculate when your eggs will go bad, preventing you from eating rotten eggs. If you wet clean your eggs, they must be stored in the fridge because you have washed off the bloom. If you dry clean the eggs, you can leave them unrefrigerated for a month. However, note that they start to lose their delicious taste after two weeks. After these two weeks pass, it is best to use freshly-laid eggs for baking or hard-boiling so that you will not notice the decline in quality and taste. Always wet wash your dry cleaned eggs before use.

If you forget to label your egg packets or you cannot recall how long your eggs have been in your kitchen, there is a simple way to test their freshness using the float test. In the float test, you simply place the eggs in a bowl filled with water. If the egg floats, it is spoiled. An egg floats when it has evaporated too much inside, causing it to have a big air pocket. If it sinks, it is okay.

You can also candle your egg to check if it is still fresh. When you candle an egg, you hold a light or candle near the egg to help you see the inside of the egg. Chicken farmers use it to check if the egg is fertile or not, but you can use it to see if the egg is still fresh. If the air sacs in the egg are large, they are not fresh. If they are small, they are fresh.

I use two simple things to candle my eggs: a bright light and a dark room. To candle an egg, simply hold a bright light up to an egg to check the size of the air sac inside. If you want to raise your own chicks, you will need to candle your eggs to check that they are fertilized and growing well. You can use the bright light and darkroom system too. To do this, carefully hold the egg up to the light, but do not look directly at the light. Hold the larger end of the egg against the light, then turn the egg slowly to see the embryo inside. Do this as quickly as possible because the light will make the embryo too hot. You must also make sure not to remove the eggs from the incubator for more than twenty to thirty minutes. If you want a more efficient and precise candling, check your local poultry or farm supply store for an egg-candling device. As a beginner backyard chicken enthusiast, it is best to wait until you have more experience before you try your hand at incubating your eggs to raise chicks.

Preparing Eggs for Sale

If you are selling your eggs, you also need to learn how to properly clean your eggs. You may get in trouble with the law if you do not take proper precautions to clean the eggs you sell. Backyard chicken enthusiasts who sell their eggs must check their county's extension office: https://nifa.usda.gov/Extension/.

Here, you can check the local and state regulations that instruct you on exactly how to clean any eggs for sale in your area. Depending on your state's laws, if your eggs are clean, you may not need to wash them. State laws vary considerably and cover issues such as labeling and grading. To avoid breaking the law, make sure you are up-to-date on the laws in your state.

You must label your egg cartons with the correct picking date before selling. It is the law because your customers will not know how long the eggs will remain fresh without it. If you want to preserve eggs for sale longer, you can use a cloth to rub the eggs with oil. The oil seals the eggs' pores, allowing them to stay protected from bacteria and air. You do not want to sell old eggs to customers, even if they are perfectly fine eggs. Your customer will want to keep the eggs in the refrigerator for a considerable period of time. If you sell them old eggs, the eggs may spoil in just a few days, and they will be disappointed in your service. You do not want to annoy (and possibly poison) a customer by selling them old eggs. This could cause your customer to report you to your local government, and they could ban you from raising chickens or, worse, be persecuted for endangering lives.

Follow every step in your local laws and regulations, including whether you need to label your eggs "ungraded" or not and whether you need to include your contact details on your eggs.

Egg Shortage and How to Correct It

If your chickens are not laying eggs or are not laying as many eggs as before, you will want to figure out why. Indeed, it is essential to know how many eggs your chickens lay daily or weekly. That way, if you see a decrease in the number of eggs they produce, you can tell immediately if something is wrong. There are many reasons why your hens will not lay eggs. As discussed in Chapter Two, it could be natural, like a change in weather, a decrease in light, or because your chickens are aging. It could also be because of other factors, like molting, poor nutrition, and stress.

Once you figure out why your chickens are producing fewer eggs, you can fix the situation immediately. Some of the reasons for egg shortages include:

. . .

Diet

Your hens' diet is often the reason why they stop laying eggs. Like humans, your chickens' diets will affect every part of their life. If they are not getting proper nutrition from a balanced diet, they will become deficient in certain nutrients and cannot lay many eggs.

If you see a decrease in egg production, try to recall if you have recently changed their brand of pellets or changed their diet in any other way. Have you stopped feeding them a particular food when you give them scraps? Did your local chicken supply store change the recipe for its chicken feed without alerting you? Did you stop adding a particular ingredient to their food, like ground-up eggshells, which provide calcium to produce new eggs? This is what one backyard chicken enthusiast (The Happy Chicken Coop, 2021) had to say:

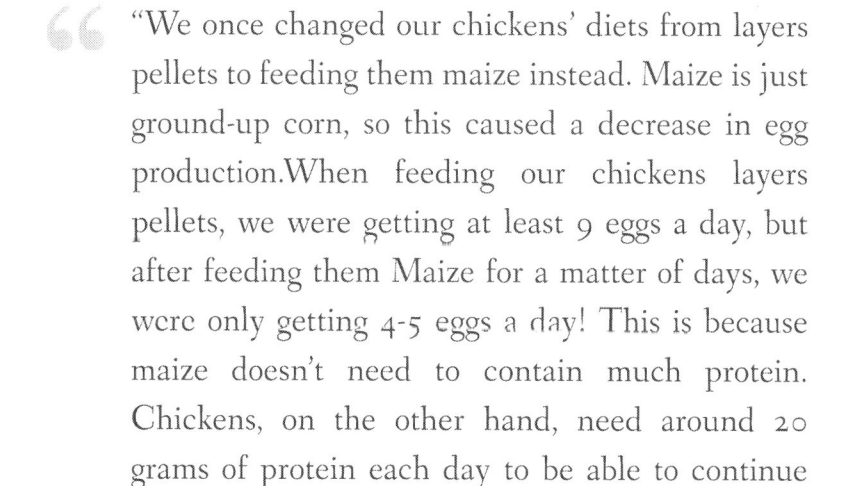

> "We once changed our chickens' diets from layers pellets to feeding them maize instead. Maize is just ground-up corn, so this caused a decrease in egg production. When feeding our chickens layers pellets, we were getting at least 9 eggs a day, but after feeding them Maize for a matter of days, we were only getting 4-5 eggs a day! This is because maize doesn't need to contain much protein. Chickens, on the other hand, need around 20 grams of protein each day to be able to continue laying eggs."

Do not forget the importance of water for a chicken (as discussed in Chapter Four). If you do not give your hens enough water, even for a few days, they will stop laying eggs. Remember to add apple cider vinegar (with the mother, which contains most of the vinegar's health benefits) to their water regularly and give them cold, freshwater when the weather is hot. All of these precautions will prevent your chicken's body from going into shock or a state of extreme stress, causing egg shortages.

It is possible to do all the above and still have egg shortages. If you feed your hens' layer pellets and follow the instructions for their water supply, then consider adding more variety into their diets by giving them snacks high in protein, such as mealworms, oats, and pumpkin seeds. If you have changed your hens' diets and see no improvement, there may be other causes.

Weather

As discussed earlier in Chapter One, hens typically lay much fewer eggs in the winter months (if you live in a colder climate). Chickens need fourteen to sixteen hours of natural daylight to lay eggs. If you so choose, you can use artificial light in their coop during colder months. However, this is often seen as unethical in the backyard chicken community. Your chickens need this time to rest and give their bodies a break. Plus, they will still lay eggs occasionally, even in the colder months.

If the weather becomes too cold, this will also affect egg production since your chickens will use all their energy to keep warm rather than produce eggs.

Breed

You already know from Chapter Three that some chicken breeds just do not lay as many eggs as others. If you have a breed that lays fewer eggs, there's nothing you can do to increase egg production.

Broodiness

Chickens are known to stop producing eggs while brooding. Chapter Three contains detailed information about broody hens and how you can resolve this problem.

New Chickens

When you introduce new chickens to the flock, it sometimes disrupts the routine of your existing community and causes them to stop laying eggs for a few days (see Chapter Five). Chickens love routine and do not like when it is disturbed. Any other disturbances to their routine can cause your chickens to stop laying eggs for a few days, including moving their coop or moving homes entirely.

. . .

Illness

Your chickens may lay very few eggs—or even none—if they are sick. Common illnesses that chickens suffer are colds, parasites, and molts. If you see sickness symptoms in any of your hens, isolate them immediately to prevent the illness from spreading among the flock.

If your chicken has a cold, she may start breathing through her mouth, leaving her mouth open at all times. She may also have slimy nostrils.

If your chick is molting, she's shedding her feathers to grow new ones. This is normal and often causes your hen to mimic symptoms of illness. Molting occurs yearly for about six to twelve weeks. Your hen will not produce eggs while she is molting.

Finally, when a hen has parasites, you will notice her scratching herself consistently. Parasites include lice, worms, and mites, and they often make chickens go pale. You can quickly treat parasites by spraying your flock and their coop with a poultry cleaner.

Stress

Stress affects chickens just like it affects humans. If your hen is very stressed, she will begin to display anxiety symptoms similar to humans. She will stop eating, stop laying eggs, lose weight, start losing feathers, and possibly even start acting in antisocial ways. A few things can cause your hens stress, like predators and a low rooster to hen ratio. If there are not enough hens for the rooster, your roosters may begin mounting your hens too often, causing stress and even bare patches on their backs and heads.

Predators could also be stealing your chickens' eggs without you knowing. As discussed in Chapter Three, use security motion sensor lights around your coop to alert you of the presence of predators. Sometimes, these predators can even be other humans stealing your eggs.

Old Age

Most hens stop producing eggs when they are three years old (see Chapter Three). If your hen is between the ages of two and three and is laying fewer eggs after you have tried everything else, then this is very likely just a case of old age.

SEVEN

CHICKEN BEHAVIOR AND TROUBLESHOOTING

"I have a farm and I love it there. There's really nothing to do, but even watching the chickens, it's fun."

-Salma Hayek

As a chicken owner, you will need to be very watchful of your chickens' behavior. The ability to spot healthy and unhealthy behavior and habits is crucial for keeping your chickens healthy. This way, you can watch for unhealthy behavior and correct these issues. Always supervise your chicken for the following behaviors so that you can spot healthiness or unhealthiness:

Dust Baths & Why They Do It

Chickens are not the only animals to take dust baths. It is a commonly observed behavior in animals like elephants, bison, zebras, and other birds.

A dust bath is as its name suggests. It is a chicken's method of cleaning themselves where they roll around in the dust in very jagged movements. To a beginner seeing a dust bath for the first time, it might resemble a seizure or a severe illness. However, just like you would with a bath, chickens use their baths to relax and clean themselves. Sometimes, they even use it to socialize.

To take a dust bath, your chicken will dig a shallow ditch in the soil, sand, mulch, or shavings; whatever finely textured material your chicken can find is good enough for a dust bath. Your chicken removes excess oil from both areas by fluffing its feathers and rubbing its skin in the dust. Dust baths are essential to a chicken's health because they eliminate parasites that could be lodging in their feathers. Parasites are very detrimental to your chicken's health (see Chapter Eight) so provide plenty of soil, sand, mulch, and safe wood shavings for your chicken to dust bath. (I prefer to use clean, dry dirt or construction-grade sand in my coop. They are the safest options for a chicken to take a dust bath.)

Dust baths also bring your chickens plenty of exercise and a way for social interaction. One backyard chicken enthusiast described it to me as chicken yoga. Plus, your chickens will cool down in hot weather by digging down into the sand to expose cooler sand. You will often see them lying down flat on the sand to cool down their bodies. After a dust bath, you will notice your chicken preening (as discussed later in this chapter).

How to Stop a Chicken from Eating Eggs

Chickens often begin eating eggs because of egg breakage. This is why you must not leave your eggs in your coop for more than one day (see Chapter Six). Despite my best efforts, I still had eggs break, even when I collected eggs twice a day. Here is what I do to further reduce my chances of egg breakage:

- I make sure there's always two-three inches of clean, dry nesting material in all of my nesting boxes. This acts as a cushion for the eggs.

- I make sure to put my fertile hens on a layer diet enriched with calcium, so their eggshells are strong. I also mix crushed eggshells into their feed so they can get more calcium. Be sure to crush the eggshells into a powder before mixing it into their feed, or your chickens will realize it is eggshells and begin to eat their eggs.

- I position the nest boxes precisely and make sure to use nest boxes of a specific dimension to ensure there is enough space for the chickens to lay eggs and move around (see Chapter Two for detailed instructions on how to position and measure your nest boxes).

- I move broody hens to another part of the coop, so they are not near the eggs constantly (see Chapter Three for dealing with a broody hen).

If one of your hens still develops a taste for eggs despite your measures, do not beat yourself up. It happens even to the most experienced of us since we cannot keep an eye on our chickens twenty-four-seven. Sometimes, your hen may be stressed and begin eating eggs as a maladaptive technique. Other times, you just have a very stubborn chicken who is determined to eat eggs. You can "break" your chickens of this habit by:

- Using roll-away nest boxes that make the egg roll away out of reach as soon as it is laid.

- Avoiding bright lights near the nesting boxes. Chickens love dark, quiet spaces for nesting (see Chapter Two).

- Not disturbing your chickens when they are in the nest laying eggs.

- Using a big enough coop and big enough nesting boxes. It would be best to also allow your chickens enough space to roam and forage every day.

- Providing fresh water and fresh feed every day. Make sure there are enough feeders and waterers for every chicken to get enough water and food.

- Placing golf balls in the nests to trick your chickens into thinking they are eggs. They will soon get tired of pecking at eggs that do not break. Chickens hate mustard, so rub mustard on the golf balls so that the chickens soon associate eggs with a disgusting taste.

Alternatively, you can create a small hole at the end of a few eggs and shake out the liquid egg. Then, squeeze yellow mustard inside the empty shell, and place the faux eggs in the nesting boxes.

Mating

If you want to incubate your eggs and sell chicks, you will need roosters. You need one rooster for every twelve hens. Hens will always choose the most attractive, healthy, and strong rooster of the bunch. They also select the roosters that can find the most food.

When a rooster wants to mate, he performs his mating behavior. He finds some food and picks it up, and drops it over and over again while clucking loudly so the hens around him can hear him. As soon as he gets their attention, he begins the chicken mating dance, which involves dropping a wing and circling the hen until she makes her choice known by either squatting in submission or walking away.

Roaming

Curiosity killed the cat, but it can also kill the chicken. Many chicken breeds are very curious. Think of them like the much-loved old lady down the street who loves to go from neighbor to neighbor to make sure everything is OK. Chickens roam because they want to know what's going on at all times. Roaming also gives them good exercise, stretches their legs, and allows them to forage simultaneously. It is perfect for the curious chicken!

Chickens like to scratch and peck at the ground while roaming. They can find a good place for a dust bath, and they can also find cool, peaceful spaces to hide their nests when they roam. Plus, like humans, chickens also need time away from each other. During the daytime, they need space away from the close quarters they spend in their coop. When you allow your chickens to roam to their hearts' content, they are less likely to be stressed, to become ill, or to engage in antisocial behavior, such as aggression. Just as you may feel much better and calm after some exercise outdoors, so do chickens.

Preening

A chicken grooms by preening. You will often see chickens cleaning themselves in large groups rather than doing it by themselves.

Preening can be said to be the equivalent of humans brushing their hair. It makes the feathers look good, keeps them in their place, and allows them to function correctly. If preened properly, the feathers insulate the chicken and keep it waterproof. A properly-preened chicken is also a well-oiled chicken. Chickens have an oil gland at the base of their tail. To oil themselves, they pick the oil gland with their beaks before preening, collecting oil to spread over their feathers.

Scratching

Scratching the ground is instinctive for chickens. There are a few reasons why a chicken scratches the ground. Scratching prepares the ground for a dust bath and reveals cooler sand or soil for the chicken to lay on. It is also theorized that scratching is a vestigial behavior passed down from their ancestors but is no longer needed. The theory states that the ancestors of chickens ate seeds and bugs just below the ground's surface. They had to scratch the earth to find these seeds and bugs.

Pecking Order

Chickens are very hierarchical animals; the strongest and the most aggressive always end up on top. If you have roosters in your flocks, they will usually form their pecking order apart from the hens, although the King Rooster will also be the leader of the hens. The hierarchy typically begins when the chickens are pullets (also known as baby chicks), but young chickens introduced to a flock have to quickly earn their place in the rank. Older chickens always establish the ranking, often staying at the top unless they are outranked by a more aggressive younger bird who successfully challenges their authority.

The pecking order is decided by pecking, chest-bumping, pushing, and stare-downs. Chickens higher on the pecking order often bully the gentler, more pacifistic chickens and can even begin to harm them if you place very gentle chicken breeds with very aggressive ones.

Helping an Egg-Bound Hen

An egg-bound hen happens very rarely, and most backyard chicken enthusiasts never experience it. However, when it happens, you must help your hen to fix the issue as soon as possible.

An egg-bound hen is a hen who is trying to lay an egg but cannot. If an egg-bound hen does not pass the egg within forty-eight hours, your chicken will die. You must know the signs of an egg-bound hen. That way, you can spot it immediately when it is happening and work to save your bird. An egg-bound hen will very likely:

- Have her eyes closed.

- Act lethargic, not move much, and prefer to sit down most of the time. When she does move around, she waddles rather than walks or struts.

- Be sitting in the corner with her feather fluffed up.

- Pump up or strain her backside. Her tail will also be down.

- Drag her wings, unable to keep them in its place.

- Not want to drink much water.

- Have liquid dripping from her vent (the opening from where she lays her eggs and releases her droppings). Her feces will also be wet.

- Have pale combs and wattles (the two red fleshy things dangling from the bottom of a chicken's head).

If you think your chicken might be egg-bound but you are uncertain, treat her as though she is anyway. As mentioned earlier, being egg-bound is fatal for a chicken, so always be very careful. If it turns out your chicken was not egg-bound, then you simply have a clean chicken at the end of the ordeal. However, one unmistakable sign of an egg-bound hen is that you will feel an egg-shaped lump inside the hen. Egg-bound hens have an egg stuck in their oviduct, the tube-like organ where they form their eggs. It is more likely for your hens to get egg-bound if they are obese, young, or forced to lay eggs all year round using artificial lighting in their coop. A hen will very likely become egg-bound if:

- She recently recovered from an illness and is still feeling weak.

- She is fed low-quality feed, or her diet has too much protein.

- Her diet is deficient in calcium, making her muscles too poorly developed to contract and expel the egg.

- Her lineage shows a history of becoming egg-bound.

- She is dehydrated.

- She has internal worms or parasites.

- She has an oviduct infection.

- She is stressed.

- She has formed a double-yolked egg or an egg that is too large and is now unable to pass it through her oviduct.

How to Treat an Egg-Bound Chicken

You must handle an egg-bound chicken with the utmost care. If you do not, the egg can break inside the hen, causing an infection and possibly death. Peritonitis is an infection that occurs when an egg breaks inside a hen. You must treat peritonitis with an antibiotic, such as Baytril, immediately. You will also have to give your hen probiotic powder to build up her good bacteria. It is a time-consuming infection to treat, so it is best to avoid it altogether.

Supplies:

- A tub of warm water

- Epsom salts

- Vegetable oil

- Liquid calcium

- Nutri-drench (a premium, nutrient-rich supplement that rapidly delivers energy and essential nutrients to a sick chicken)

- A crate or box

Directions:

Soak her in warm water: Gently bring the hen into your house. Place a small plastic tub in your bathtub, then fill it with warm water with some Epsom salts. Carefully place the hen into the tub to soak, ensuring that the water covers her lower body and vent. Soak her in the tub for about twenty minutes, gently rubbing her abdomen. Then, remove her carefully from the rub and gently towel dry her by blotting her feathers with care.

If it is cold or windy, use a hairdryer on a low setting to dry her instead.

Lubricate and massage her vent: After this, rub some vegetable oil around her vent and gently massage her abdomen.

Create moist heat: Place your hen in a quiet and dark location—preferably in a large crate or cage. You can create a quiet, dark area for your chicken by layering some towels and blankets inside a dog or birdcage. You can layer towels that have been warmed in the dryer at the bottom to keep your bird warmer for longer. You can even place a heating pad or hot water bottle under the layers of a towel, making sure the top does not get too hot for your chicken. If you have a heat lamp, you can also use it to warm your chicken. You want to create moist heat, so place a pan of hot water somewhere in the room, too, close to the chicken.

Administer a calcium supplement and Nutri-drench: Give your hen an eyedropper full of Nutri-drench. Then administer one cc of liquid calcium.

Leave your chicken to rest by herself for a while, repeating the soak in the tub every hour until she finally lays the egg.

Extract the egg yourself: If you can see the egg, but your chicken is still not able to push it out after a few hours, it is best to take your chicken to a vet. Some backyard chicken enthusiasts try to extract the egg themselves, but this is a dangerous procedure that can be fatal if your chicken becomes infected.

To extract the egg yourself, you will need to see the egg in the chicken's vent. Use a syringe to gently remove the contents of the egg. Then carefully crush the egg's shell, ensuring that the fragments stay attached to the membrane. Rub vegetable oil around the shell and the vent before gently removing the shell. If you try to do this procedure and it does not work successfully, take your chicken to the vet immediately.

How to Prevent Your Hens from Becoming Egg-Bound

- Feed them the best-quality feed.

- Do not use artificial lighting during the winter months to increase egg production.

- Feed your chickens crushed eggshells and oyster shells regularly and give them the option to eat as much as they need.

- Give your chickens healthy treats and scraps infrequently.

- Ensure they have plenty of space in your backyard to roam and exercise.

EIGHT

HEALTH CONCERNS AND REMEDIES

"If I didn't start painting, I would have raised chickens."

-William Lyon Phelps

You will need to be able to spot common chicken diseases and parasites so that you can take care of your chickens if they become infected.

Chicken First-Aid Kit

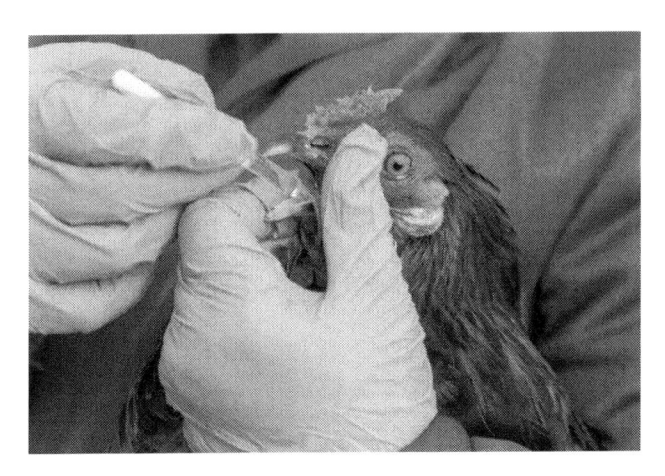

Always keep a chicken first-aid kit in your home. You never know when one of your chickens will run into a health emergency, such as fighting a predator or sudden illness. Depending on where you live, it can also take a while to reach your vet, so a first-aid kit can help keep your chicken alive in the meantime.

Your first-aid kit should contain the following:

- Rubbing alcohol

- Rubber gloves

- Eyedropper or syringe (for hand-feeding water, medications, and liquid nutrients to a sick chicken)

- Vitamins and electrolytes (for dehydration, shock, and heat stress)

- Vet wrap

- Non-stick gauze pads

- Blu Kote

- Scissors

- Neosporin (with no pain reliever in it)

- Blood stop powder

- Corid (to treat coccidiosis)

- Dog or cat nail trimmers (for trimming beaks and toenails)

- Styptic powder (for bleeding nails or beaks).

- Tweezers

- LED flashlight

- Wazine (to treat worms)

- Epsom salt

- Vetericyn

- Self-sticking bandages

Caring for a Sick or Injured Chicken

There are a few steps to caring for a sick or injured chicken. Knowing all the steps before an emergency is like building a first-aid kit before a crisis. You will be able to effectively take care of your chicken if you learn all the steps before your chicken gets sick. (Always wear gloves when handling an ill chicken to prevent getting infected yourself.)

Isolate the sick chicken: Isolating a chicken immediately after you spot signs of illness (see Chapter Five) will prevent infections and diseases from spreading to the other chickens. It will also prevent the weak and sick chicken from being injured by the others. If you wrap the chicken loosely in a large towel, they are less fussy when you move them away from their flock.

Stop any bleeding: If there is any bleeding, stop it immediately. Use a clean towel, gauze, or paper towel to stop the bleeding by firmly pressing it on the injured area until the bleeding stops. You can also stop bleeding by using blood stop powder on more minor, shallower wounds.

Take care of any injuries immediately: Always examine the chicken from head to toe because chicken feathers can hide injuries. A bath will help you find any injuries more quickly. If you find a wound, pluck or trim the feathers around the wound so you can access the wound properly. Do not pluck or cut the feather if they are pin feathers. A pin feather is a new feather that is just emerging during molting. They are very fragile and are even supplied with blood. If you pluck or trim it, your chicken will begin to bleed. You can tell a feather is a pin feather coated with a wax-like substance called epitrichium.

Wash any wounds on your chicken's body very well with water, then spray non-alcoholic wound care spray. An alcohol-based antiseptic and antifungal wound spray may hurt the chicken a lot.

After you do this, always keep the wound clean and dry until your hen heals. Watch out for signs of infections, such as redness or swelling in the wound area.

Administer supplements and electrolytes: Your chicken may be shocked by their illness or injury. Add vitamins and electrolytes to her water for a few days to help her build her strength back up. Never give a chicken electrolytes for more than three days because it will weaken them.

Give food and water: Water is more critical to an ill chicken than food, so give your sick chicken plenty of water. Your chicken uses water to regulate its metabolism and body temperature, digest food, and eliminate body waste. If your chicken is too sick to drink, use an eyedropper to feed her water.

Try to feed your bird because she will need the energy to heal. If she cannot eat on her own after twenty-four hours, use an eyedropper or syringe to feed her liquid Nutri-drench.

Administer anti-inflammatory and pain medication: Chickens do not often show signs that they are in pain. They are very stoic animals because showing signs of distress will usually attract predators. If there are no internal injuries, add five 65 mg tablets of aspirin to one gallon of water. Feed your chicken this water for three days to ensure she is not in any pain.

Call the vet: If your chicken is not responding to treatment, or her condition deteriorates, she may need antibiotics, or she may have an internal injury. You cannot help a chicken with an internal injury; only a vet can help.

Return the chicken to the flock: Chickens have been known to pick on injured and sick chickens. They have even been known to cannibalize injured or recovering chickens. This is why you must never return a chicken to the flock until she has shown full recovery. If there are any visible scabs or blood on the chicken when you return her to the community, you are placing your chicken's life in danger.

When it is time to reintroduce your healed chicken to the flock, introduce her like she is a new chicken, using the strategies in Chapter Five.

Common Chicken Diseases and Parasites

There are a few common diseases and parasites that infect chickens. Knowing how to prevent and stop them will help you keep a healthy flock. Some of these diseases have already been discussed in previous chapters and segments. Similarly, preventing diseases and parasites has been discussed extensively in earlier chapters of this book.

In previous chapters, you have learned how to spot and treat the following conditions:

- Egg-laying problems (Chapters six and seven).

- Pasty vent (Chapter five).

- Cuts and wounds (Chapter eight).

Other infections and parasites to watch out for are:

Viral Diseases: Viral diseases are severe if left untreated. Furthermore, they are very contagious and can easily infect your whole flock if you do not detect them early. They are also often difficult to treat. They include avian flu, fowl pox, infectious bronchitis, Marek's disease, and Newcastle disease.

These are some symptoms that show that your chicken may be suffering a viral infection: coughing or sneezing, sores on the skin, declined egg production, nasal and eye discharge, and even paralysis. For example, the symptoms of avian flu include diarrhea, swollen comb and wattles, purple discoloration, nasal discharge, coughing and sneezing, swelling, and ruffled feathers. Viral infections can be prevented by giving your chicks their vaccinations. Most chicken breeders vaccinate their chicks before selling them to others.

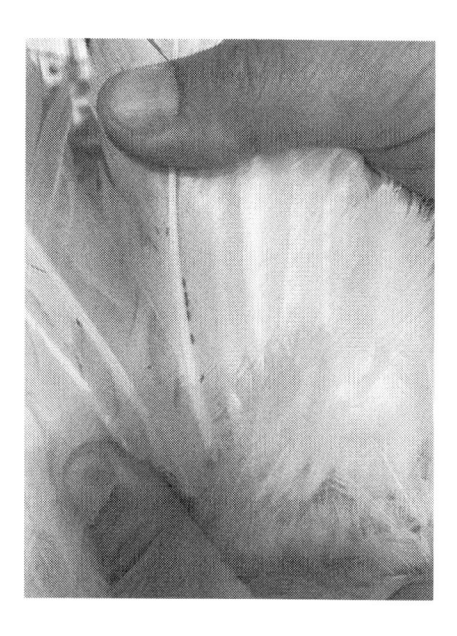

Parasitic Diseases: Parasitic diseases are often caused by lice, mites, worms, and ticks (lice are pictured in this photo). If you do not clean your coop and the bedding regularly, your chickens will get parasitic infections. Do not buy a second-hand coop—they are often riddled with parasitic insects. Spray insecticides in your coop regularly. Parasitic illnesses are usually loss of appetite, feather loss, lethargy, and skin irritation. If one of your chickens has lice, mites, worms, or ticks, treat her with antiparasitic medications and supplements.

Bacterial Diseases: Although they are not common, bacterial diseases are very contagious and can kill your entire flock quickly. Once you find the chicken carrying the bacteria, you will have to separate it from the flock immediately and put it down. Bacterial diseases that affect your chickens include salmonellosis (caused by salmonella), colibacillosis (caused by E. coli), and chronic respiratory diseases.

Unlike baby chicks, older chickens do not show any symptoms of salmonellosis. This is why you must keep your coop well-cleaned and well-maintained at all times to reduce your risk of any chicken catching a bacterial infection. Colibacillosis and chronic respiratory disease symptoms include chickens no longer producing eggs, respiratory and breathing issues, and a swollen face and sinuses.

Fungal Diseases: Fungal infections are also very rare in chickens. Luckily, they are easy to treat, too. If they do get a fungal infection, it is typically either ringworms or brooder pneumonia. Brooder pneumonia affects young chicks by causing respiratory problems and breathing issues. Ringworms often clear up on their own because they are so mild. You will know a chicken is infected with ringworm when it has a thick, white layer on its comb (see below).

Foot injuries: Foot injuries are not as life-threatening as the other illnesses and injuries that a chicken can get. However, they are challenging to treat.

Foot injuries are usually caused by a small cut on the chicken's foot. It is not life-threatening unless it becomes infected. Your chicken may also get a staph infection, which is another cause of a foot injury called bumblefoot (see below).

If your chicken is not placing weight on one foot or has completely stopped walking, this is a sign that she probably has an injured foot. Simply apply wound wash to the injured foot and then bandage it lightly to prevent further infection.

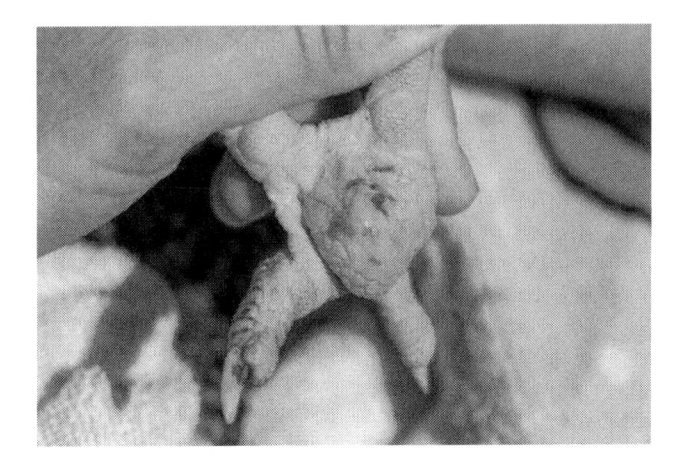

To make your own saline wound wash, mix 100 ml of filtered or boiled water with ⅛ teaspoon, non-iodized salt, and ¼ teaspoon baking soda in a sterile container. It keeps well in the fridge for two days if the bottle is lidded. Remember to always keep injured hens away from the rest of the flock until they are completely healed.

If your chicken has bumblefoot, use an antiseptic wound wash, cream, and gauze. If this does not heal the foot, you will have to take your chicken to the vet to drain the abscess.

PLEASE REVIEW MY BOOK
YOU CAN MAKE A DIFFERENCE

Enjoy this book? You can make a huge difference!

Reviews are the most powerful tool for authors when it comes to getting attention for our books! As much as I would love to have tons of money to throw at advertising I'm simply not there yet.

However... loyal readers such as yourself can make all the difference. Honest reviews of my book help bring them to the attention of other readers.

If you enjoyed my book I would be grateful if you would spend just five minutes leaving a review (as short or as long as you want it to be!) You can do so by simply clicking the following link or typing it into your desktop: https://www.amazon.com/Raising-Backyard-Chickens-Beginners-Production-ebook/dp/B0989P4MFK/ref=sr_1_1?dchild=1&key-

words=B0989P4MFK&qid=1635904241&qsid=137-0858384-9836022&sr=8-1&sres=B0989P4MFK

Thank you so much for you time!

FINAL WORDS

"I just love chickens."

-Patti LuPone

You are about to do one of the most rewarding things a person can do! You are about to raise chickens! Congratulate yourself on being a responsible and caring bird raiser. You care about raising healthy, happy chickens, so you pored through this book, searching for extensive detailed advice on how to do so.

With the knowledge you have acquired from this book, you now know that you will be great at raising chickens! You can already picture the different breeds strutting around in your backyard with their beautiful feathers, clucking happily in search of bugs and grit. You may already be able to visualize the exact coop that you want in your yard and the specific breeds you plan to keep. You are now one step closer to living the idyllic life of raising animals for food and companionship. Even better, you are about to make some new friends and build lasting bonds with your chickens.

As you begin making plans to raise backyard chickens, remember the most important thing: do not stress. This is supposed to be about having fun, trying something new, and living a lifestyle that's closer to nature and better for your health. Remember that the more proximity you have with nature and animals, the less stress you will feel. This is no reason to be nervous. Remind yourself that you are embarking on a relaxing and stress-free journey.

The advice and information in this book are a lot to remember for a beginner. I would recommend bookmarking essential pages for easy reference. Do not be afraid to make mistakes.

Even the most seasoned backyard chicken enthusiast makes mistakes. Keep trying and surround yourself with a support group of the same hobbyists. You may be able to find a backyard chicken support group in your local community. If not, why not think about starting one? And you will be able to find support groups online too. I recommend joining our Facebook community: Living a Sustainable Independent Lifestyle Community.

You may now be deciding on what feeders to buy what delicious cakes your eggs will bake. Dream on and plan on, but do not forget an essential and fun step: naming your birds. Yes, you will need to choose names for all your birds. I recommend that you always select names based on their personalities and appearance.

There may be a "Miss Bossy-Boots," "Mr. Big-Beard," and a "Mrs. Carrot Cake". You have already committed to raising a flock, so why not have fun naming them too? Simply be prepared to raise a few eyebrows when your neighbors, friends, and family hear you shouting at "Mr. Hot Stuff" for bullying "Mrs. Carrot Cake".

If you enjoyed this book, please leave a comment and a star rating on Amazon or Audible! Your reviews help others find this book. Thank you so much for reading!

ALSO BY DANIEL A. HART

Raising Goats: A Beginner's Guide to a Healthy Herd, Milk Production and Quality Home Grown Meat

ABOUT THE AUTHOR

Daniel A. Hart currently lives in Iowa with his family on a small farm just outside the city. He stays very busy between family, daily life on the farm and running his construction company. He was raised in an Amish community where he learned many valuable traits and tools for living off the land and providing for yourself. He has always had a passion for writing and felt compelled to share his years of experience in hopes to aid others in their sustainable journey.

For more information:
daniel@daniel-hart.com

REFERENCES

Anderson, K.E. (2011). Comparison Of Fatty Acid, Cholesterol, And Vitamin A And E Composition In Eggs From Hens Housed In Conventional Cage And Range Production Facilities. *Poultry Science.* 90(7), pp. 1600–8.

Backyard Chickens. (2021). Home. Retrieved from: https://www.backyardchickens.com/.

Clauer, P.J. (2021). Small Scale Poultry Housing. Retrieved from https://www.pubs.ext.vt.edu/content/dam/pubs_ext_vt_edu/2902/2902-1092/2902-1092_pdf.pdf.

Elise. (2017). Free Ranging Chickens: The Pros And Cons. Retrieved from https://www.scoopfromthecoop.com/pros-and-cons-of-free-ranging-chickens/.

Elkhoraibi, C., Blatchford, R.A., Pitesky, M.E. & Mench, J.A. (2014). Backyard Chickens In The United States: A Survey Of Flock Owners. *Poultry Science.* 93(11), pp. 2920-31. https://pubmed.ncbi.nlm.nih.gov/25193256/.

Freedom Ranger Hatchery, Inc. (2021). What to Feed Your Chickens, and What Not to Feed Them. Retrieved from https://www.freedomrangerhatchery.com/blog/what-to-feed-your-chickens-and-what-not-to-feed-them/.

Kelly. (2012). Pros And Cons Of Backyard Chickens. Retrieved from https://onceamonthmeals.com/blog/series/get-real/pros-and-cons-of-backyard-chickens/.

National Institute Of Food And Agriculture. (2021). Extension. Retrieved from https://nifa.usda.gov/Extension/.

Newport Academy. (2021). 10 Ways Pets Support Mental Health. Retrieved from https://www.newportacademy.com/resources/well-being/pets-and-mental-health/.

Pointdexter, J. (2021). Identifying 14 Common Chicken Predators (And How To Protect Them). Retrieved from https://morningchores.com/chicken-predators/.

Statista. (2021). Broiler Meat Production Worldwide In 2021, By Country (In 1,000 Metric Tons). Retrieved from https://

www.statista.com/statistics/237597/leading-10-countries-worldwide-in-poultry-meat-production-in-2007/.

Texas A&M Agrilife Extension. (2010). Backyard Hens. Retrieved from https://bexar-tx.tamu.edu/files/2012/06/Backyard-Basics-Chickens.pdf.

The Happy Chicken Coop. (2021). 7 Reasons Why Your Chickens Stopped Laying Eggs. Retrieved from https://www.thehappychickencoop.com/7-reasons-why-your-chickens-stopped-laying-eggs/.

Printed in Great Britain
by Amazon